Vüe du Village de CHELSEA.

intseller, near Serjeants Inn Fleet Street.

To
Lucy, Henry
and Edward

Also by Ysenda Maxtone Graham

The Church Hesitant

The Real Mrs Miniver

Mr Tibbits's Catholic School

An Insomniac's Guide to the Small Hours

Also by Zebedee Helm

The Middle Class ABC

Kit and Willy's Dogs of the World

Maggie and Rose's Lovely Story

Oscar and Bentley are Heroes and Totally Save the Day

The Story of Cameron House School

by Ysenda Maxtone Graham

Cheerfully illustrated by
Zebedee Helm

DA MIHI SAPIENTIAM

Published by Cameron House School Publishing 2014
Printed and bound in the UK by
The Wren Press, 1 Curzon Street, London W1J 5HD
© 2014 Ysenda Maxtone Graham, Zebedee Helm and Cameron House School Publishing
Designed by Katrina ffiske

Etching credit: J. Maurer, *A View of Chelsea*, 1744,
by kind permission of Kensington Central Library.

ISBN 978-0-9928667-0-9

www.cameronhouseschool.org

Contents

Foreword
by Josie Cameron Ashcroft

This book is dedicated to my three children, Lucy, Henry and Edward, each of whom has asked me over the years, 'How did Cameron House School begin?' What follows is nothing more than a merry, light-hearted romp through the decades, and I hope it will enlighten them just a little as to how the school came into being. Was it making and teaching wooden peg dolls in a miniature classroom set inside a shoebox in the garden in Dunedin, or was it teaching children on the eighth floor in an attic in Cadogan Gardens in London?

Having also had numerous requests over the years from Friends of Cameron House who were curious too, I called in the author Ysenda Maxtone Graham, who interviewed copious numbers of Old Cameronians, parents and staff, as well as some from the present day, each of whom related to her something of life at the school as they recalled it over the decades – both pre- and après the invention of Health and Safety risk assessments and financial management accounts. She chatted to people across the globe, starting in Chelsea,

Kensington, the Square Mile and Hackney, and fanning out (by telephone, Facebook and Skype) to France, South Africa, New York, San Francisco and Malaysia. Each person she spoke to brought a vital patch of detail and colour to the overall picture; Ysenda and I are both deeply grateful to everyone who has spared time to speak to her and thus to make this book come to life.

Zebedee Helm, whose wonderful work with *The Spectator*, and his children's books, all took a back seat while he worked his illustrative magic, has brought alive in pictorial form many vivid memories of the journey from that shoebox to the verger's cottage behind St Luke's Church, which led to *that* redbrick building.

Introduction

'D'you know, she arrived in Britain from New Zealand in the 1970s with nothing but a backpack?' That was the first biographical detail I heard about Josie Cameron Ashcroft. Instantly I longed to know more. Who was this New Zealander with a backpack, and how did she manage, out of said backpack, to grow Cameron House, a school which, four decades later, is one of the most vibrant small independent schools in central London? The image of Josie as a kind of Mary Poppins figure kept coming into my mind, as I imagined her opening the backpack and pulling out a fully formed redbrick school in Chelsea, complete with children's scooters lined up on the front steps.

As I later learned from talking to her, she did and still does indeed have a Mary Poppins-ish 'can do' attitude to life. Though there was no actual magic involved, there were lots of near-miraculous meetings and serendipitous coincidences which made it possible for her school to come into being. There was also a tracking incident worthy of the CIA, in the pre-mobile phone and internet era, when Josie undertook single-handedly to search the whole of Australia for the two elusive human beings without whose signatures 4 The Vale could not pass into her ownership...and it was already July...and she had promised parents that the school would open in September…and the building needed extensive refurbishment. Did she manage to track them down, and, if so, how, exactly? Read on.

As we London parents search websites and prospectuses to choose the right school for our children, it's easy to forget that schools like Cameron House don't just come into being of their own volition. The founding of an independent school requires one person's (or a small group of people's) vision, energy, willpower and courage. As anyone with a lazy streak in their character knows, it's tempting to let other people do the difficult things like founding and running schools. We'll just try to get our children into them: that's quite difficult enough, thank you. Josie is someone who has always made things happen, not taken 'no' for an answer, led from the front, and brought other people on board to help her to turn her ideals and visions into reality.

I hadn't imagined, as I set out to research the history of Cameron House, that in order to discover more about the person arriving in Britain with the backpack I would find myself reading from cover to cover the dry and formal history of the school which Josie herself attended. But I did. It was the 1959 black-and-white photographs of girls in kilts (one of them young Josie, good as gold in the Infant Room) which drew me in. On the other side of the world, in what can only be described as Scottish New Zealand, Josie went daily to Columba Girls' College, Dunedin, dressed in Hunting McKinnon tartan. Cameron House girls wear kilts. Is this significant? I wanted to find out; so I hope the reader will forgive me if we go on a short trip to New Zealand at the beginning of this book to look for Josie's origins and formation.

'I'm a visual person,' Josie has said to me often. 'Images are as important and evocative as words.' Her way of telling me about the

richness and variety of Cameron House life has been as much through photographs as through words, though her verbal accounts have been vivid and scholarly. She has shown me collages of photographs of the school's early days, and she remembers the names of each pupil ('such a lovely child,' she has often said, and meant it). I've lost count of the number of photographs of Josie and her pioneer staff I've seen, dressed in pie-crust collars, pearls and Alice bands, as so many of us were in the 1980s. I've also seen numerous photographs of her pupils through the decades, smiling the smiles of fulfilled schoolchildren. But in her choice of domain name for her email address, Josie displays prowess with words. It is '@adesk'.

We all work at desks. All of our email addresses could be 'us@adesk'. But Josie's desk is of particular significance. Her career as a helper of children with dyslexia took root in a corridor of the very earliest Thomas's School in Cadogan Gardens. In that corridor, Josie was given a rickety old desk to teach at. That desk was the small object out of which the whole of Cameron House was to grow.

Chapter 1
The Other Side of the World

'Happy, happy girls of Columba, who will ever associate this sunny hill top and this stately pile with the morning and springtime of their lives.' Thus wrote the Revd W. Gray Dixon, one of the founders of Columba Girls' College, Dunedin, in 1915, the year it was established.

Just reading and hearing about Josie's childhood school (where she went from 1959 to 1970) makes you feel ruddy-cheeked with New Zealand-Scottish fresh air. 'My great-grandparents, Camerons of Lochiel, were crofters,' Josie said. 'They sailed across the globe and went all the way round New Zealand until they found somewhere identical to Scotland.' This must have been the case for many, because a whole mini-Scotland was established in this place, complete with a Presbyterian place of worship called Knox Church. Here are more words from the Revd W. Gray Dixon, who could just as easily be describing Edinburgh or Dundee as Dunedin: 'The school building is a noble structure, worthy to be an ancient manor house among the historic Scottish hills, with its stone walls, in places three feet thick, its pointed gables, its lordly porch bedecked with ivy and covered with a carved coat of arms and its handsomely laid out grounds.'

What were the school's houses called? Iona, Braemar, Girton and Solway. 'I was in Iona,' Josie said. 'Thank goodness, because our badge was blue, which was my favourite colour.' (All her life, Josie has felt strongly about colours. It would later take two years of discussions with the Peter Jones uniform department to get them to design a uniform for Cameron House whose colours were cheerful enough to please her.) As for the Columba Girls' College kilts, they were all the dull-red and dark green of the Hunting McKinnon tartan. 'It was a proper pleated kilt,' Josie said. 'The full eight yards of material. It swung beautifully. A man called Mr McAlistair came from Scotland with his team to manage the kilts for the whole school. At the start of term you had to kneel down to make sure your kilt just touched the floor.'

'Did you have any feeling that you yourself would one day be running a school?' I asked Josie.

'Not at all! I don't think you were expected to think of a career. You'd perhaps hope to get a job till you were married at 23.'

'So, what were your dreams and hopes at that stage?'

'I did dream of expanding my horizons, of exploring new opportunities and of creating something new, something "out of my box".'

Columba Girls' College's first principal, Miss Ross, gave this address at the school's founding in 1915: 'In a girls' college of this kind the first and chief place will be given to the study of the Book of Books, which is able to make them wise unto salvation. Moral education must have its basis in religion. It has been well said that the soul of all culture is the culture of the soul. The training of each girl to full and perfect womanhood must ever be the ideal we have before us. Any intrusion into her education of mere intellectuality as an aim is wrong to herself and to the community.'

Though the school had modernised considerably, these basic tenets were still in place in the 1950s and '60s. There was at least one religious service per day, and regular Bible class at Knox Church. 'The boys from McGlashan Boys' College had to pipe us into church,' Josie recalls. 'My brother was head of the pipe band, as well as captain of the First XV.'

When Josie talks about her schooldays, you sense that she was someone who enjoyed and respected the rules and traditions, but also slightly wanted to push against them. She was a girl full of energy, whose horizons were never going to stop at being a housewife in Dunedin. Here she is on the subject of felt hats: 'The badge on our felt hat had to be facing forward at a very particular angle. We'd get a detention if any parts of our uniform were missing or twisted, and that included the dainty beige gloves and double-breasted green blazers, which had to be fully buttoned when we arrived at school in the morning and when we left in the evening. One day I got cross about the silly rule about hat-angles and sat on my hat on purpose and twisted it. I had to steam it back into shape. The highlight of the decade was when Princess Anne came to visit the school in the early 1960s. Talk about steaming hats!'

'How exactly do you steam a hat?' I asked.

'You put on an asbestos glove and hold the hat above the steam that's gushing from a kettle.'

This was one of the many practical skills that Josie acquired as a schoolgirl. Life-saving, which the girls were taught to do in Dunedin's Olympic-sized swimming-pool, was another. When Josie recalls the life-saving lessons in her early teens, she blushes at one particular memory – a memory that perhaps embarrasses her whole Columba Girls' College peer group. 'Our life-saving textbook came from England and it was pretty out-of-date, but we had to obey it to the letter. We had to swim six lengths wearing clothes precisely specified in the textbook: it had to be a fully buttoned-up blouse, a fully gathered skirt with a zip and a button on the waistband, and stockings and suspenders. Well, Dunedin wasn't exactly cosmopolitan, but we were up with the times enough to be wearing tights by 1967. But no, tights were not what the textbook said. So we had to go to the very old-fashioned shop in Dunedin called Penrose's – a shop where they put the customer's cash in a small barrel and it shot up into pipes along the ceiling to the accounts department – and say, "Er, I'd like to buy a suspender belt." Can you imagine how embarrassing that was?'

Josie was the middle child of five children in a happy family, who lived within walking distance of the school. Her father had a farm – a farm so big that he travelled across it in his small plane, a Cessna 150. 'Flying was his great passion,' Josie said. 'My mother had run the Dunedin children's library before her marriage. But in New Zealand in those days, once a woman married she never took a paid job again. She would walk us down to the local library every Saturday morning. We always read a lot.'

'Did you ever travel beyond the shores of the South Island?'

'Never! I never took any public transport at all until I left school – unless you count a coach I once took on a school trip to Oamaru.'

School holidays were spent in Dunedin, climbing trees, collecting crabs from the river, swimming, playing tennis and fives on the McGlashan school's courts and making clothes. 'We all made our own clothes,' Josie said. It was almost unheard of to go into a clothes shop and buy a ready-made dress. 'We imported Vogue "dress sewing patterns" from England and made them on our sewing machines. We had mannequin parades. We practised for the school show walking down catwalks with books on our heads to help excellent deportment.'

As a very young child Josie used to get clothes pegs off the washing line and turn them into beautiful dolls. 'I used to borrow my mother's biggest crystal sandwich plates and make miniature country scenes with moss. Or find an old shoebox and make it into a doll's house.' Do we see the beginnings of a creative teacher of children? Josie told me that she still loves doll's houses today. 'I have three of them at my house in Oxford, plus two doll's shops.' In quiet moments she can still be found putting tiny Brussels sprouts into the Aga where they will shrink (with any luck) to doll's house-size.

It was weird, Josie said, when the family acquired its first television in the early 1960s. 'It encroached on your life. Suddenly you were

expected to sit still and watch a screen.' This didn't come naturally to Josie. 'I wasn't really interested. But I was terrified of *Doctor Who*, and used to hide behind the sofa at the very sight and sound of the Daleks.'

Every day of her 11 years (33 terms) at Columba Girls' College, Josie had the same packed lunch: a Vegemite and lettuce sandwich, a boiled egg, an apple, and a kiwi fruit – 'which used to be known as a Chinese gooseberry,' she remembers. Cameron House children bring in their own packed lunches and Josie approves of the simplicity and lack of fuss which this entails. A few privileges were introduced as the Columba girls went up the school. In the Sixth Form prefects were allowed to toast bread over the log fire in the Prefects' Study. 'We were continually burning everything in sight. I still love burnt toast: it reminds me of all the fun.' (In the early days of The Learning Tree in Chelsea, there were to be one or two memorable burnt-toast incidents.)

'Did you have any male teachers at Columba?' I asked her.

'No, our teachers were all women. The only man was the chaplain.'

Josie was not starved of male company, however, as she had brothers, who went to McGlashan. 'In my last year at school I secretly got a job in the corner shop,' Josie said. 'My parents didn't know. I was bored, and wanted to do something, get out there. There were trays and trays of sweets, just like in a sweet shop in a Roald Dahl story – and my job was to fill them. We also sold ice-creams and had to dip them into hot chocolate sauce. If any McGlashan boys I liked came in, I gave their ice-cream a double-dip. With my first pay-cheque I bought a huge radio cassette player, so big that I had to ask someone to carry it home.' She bought cassettes of Pink Floyd, Led Zeppelin and Black Sabbath. 'My musical tastes are hugely diverse these days,' she reassured me. 'Nowadays I'm more of a Tallis-Bach-Mozart-Wagner-

8

Satie type of person. I love classical music and listen to it a lot – though I still adore my '60s LPs.'

With her second pay-cheque she bought some hot pants. Not just any hot pants: purple suede ones. But she still had to wear Columba College 'Sunday attire' for church: a bottle-green velvet dress gathered at the waist ('every teenage girl's nightmare') with little velvet buttons all the way down the front in groups of five, all topped off with cream lace at the collar and cuffs. And for her first ball, she had to wear a cream dress with puffed sleeves made by her mother's dressmaker, and long white gloves.

In order to prepare for these formal dances, the Columba girls were given ballroom dancing lessons by the ballroom dancing instructor who was – surprisingly – a man. At first, the lessons were girls-only. The girls were paired together in height order. 'I was lucky,' Josie said, 'because I was only just over 5ft tall, so I always got the female role, whereas the taller girls had to take the male role.' As the girls got better at the

9

a crescent?   a croissant

dances, it was decided that they were ready to progress to the next level. 'At this point the scarring images arrive,' Josie said, remembering 'a whole busload of McGlashan boys, all in the sixth form too, who would be brought in so we could practise with "the real thing" – boys. The dancing master folded his arms, stood back, and told the boys to go and collect a girl. We would all be cowering along the sides of the hall, praying that the staff had got the boy/girl ratio right, and dreading being the wallflower if there was an odd one out.'

As soon as she left school, Josie took steps towards becoming a teacher. She did a teacher-training course and a degree course in French at the same time, and got a Diploma of Education and a Certificate of Teaching. She was awarded a scholarship to go and study French in Nouméa, the capital of the French island territory of New Caledonia, and here her eyes were opened and her passionate thirst for travel was born. 'I spent six weeks of the summer of 1972 on that island in the Pacific. It was the first time I'd ever left New Zealand. It was a turning point. It was wonderful: so richly diverse! We went out on boats to the lighthouse. I stayed in the Embassy. I'd never seen such glamorous dresses – and you could get them from a shop, not a dressmaker! You could actually see what things looked like before they were made!'

She saw (and tasted) her first-ever croissant, her first-ever baguette. She loved the market, overflowing with colourful fruit. 'Our food in New Zealand was wholesome and plain. All this colour made me long to spread my wings and see more of the world.'

Back in Dunedin, she started applying for teaching jobs; and she was lucky. 'I could have been sent to the back of beyond. But I got a job at a state school called Mairangi Bay, in the trendiest part of Auckland, on the North Shore. I'd never even been to the North Island before. It's a completely different climate. I drove myself up there in my Morris 1100 with my canoe on the roof-rack. I got a job as a class teacher of 45 seven- to eight-year-old boys and girls.' She was twenty.

At once she got to work making a little world for her pupils to thrive in. From the very beginning of her teaching career, there seems to have been a driving force inside her to banish the dreariness and scariness of schools, to bring colour and warmth to where many children had found only drabness and coldness.

'I turned an area of the classroom into a beautiful reading corner, and I bought a swinging basket which I asked my boyfriend to put up for me, so I could sit with a child on each side of me and read to them. I made a post-box so the children could write letters to each other, to help the ones who weren't motivated. I had made a rickety fence and a gate to enclose the new reading and library corner: there'd probably be some reason why that wouldn't be allowed today – it would be deemed

a Health and Safety risk. In another corner I had fish bowls. I made macramé roping to hold the bowls one on top of the other, stacked five high. The children would look at them and write wonderful stories and poems about the fish. A child would bring in a bird's nest, and we'd spend time talking about it. Or someone would ask about Inuit igloos, and that would be the topic for the whole morning – we'd even create maths questions about igloos. I loved teaching. You could use your imagination every day, and you always had to keep on your toes because there were so many children with different needs.'

Geoff was the name of the boyfriend, 'an accountant, a lovely chap'. Josie's memories of her free time are all of sunshine, water, wilderness and fun. 'We used to go heli-tubing together – you pump up inner tube tyres and go whizzing down miles and miles of river. And we did white-water rafting, and canoeing and scuba-diving. And a lot of tramping as well: going off into the bush with a backpack for two or three days, finding water in the rivers. Once we had to make a stretcher out of a rimu tree, to carry an injured member of the tramping party. It was the only tree around with a straight trunk.' In quieter moments she would hand crochet maxi shawls and sell them at the market. 'I was hyperactive,' she admits. 'There was such a rich and wonderful

14

cosmopolitan atmosphere in Auckland, people pouring in from other places.'

She taught at the school for three years. But something was impending, and that was the sense that she was heading slowly but surely towards marriage. 'I felt too young to marry. I just knew I wasn't ready. And the only way I could get away from marrying Geoff was to say I wanted to get some OE.'

I thought she meant by this, 'I wanted to acquire an Old Etonian,' but she corrected me. 'OE' is what New Zealanders who long to spread their wings call 'overseas experience'. Josie wanted to make her way across the world to Europe and England. She went and bought a green canvas backpack from the tramping shop. That was THE backpack.

the backpack

Chapter 2
'Does England Look Like Coronation Street?'

Thus it was that, having taken no public transport throughout the whole of her childhood and teens, Josie changed tack completely, setting off over sea and land and hopping onto dodgy-looking long-distance buses across a variety of unknown and exotic Asian countries.

'Did your parents approve of this?' I asked her.

'My father had died when I was seventeen. My mother was not exactly thrilled, let's put it that way,' Josie said. 'There was no ill-feeling; just a lack of understanding. "Why would you want to do that?" was her reaction.'

It was 1978. Josie travelled with two other girls. 'At Singapore we joined an overland bus which took us all the way to India and on to the Kashmir region, where we stayed in houseboats. I'd met two Australian geography teachers, lovely chaps, and we hitched and took trains across Pakistan, Afghanistan and Iran. On the train to Rawalpindi I dressed up as a man so I could sit in the men's railway carriage rather than in the livestock carriage where the women were, but I was caught and arrested. I was in prison for two days. Later we were stuck for days at

the border from Iran to Iraq, waiting to get across. I got bored and drew hopscotch squares in the sand, and before you knew it the border guards were doing hopscotch in the sand with us.'

Anyone who has worked with Josie in the decades since would recognise her in that scene. Someone who can get an Iranian border guard to do hopscotch is someone who has a gift for getting people onto her side.

They travelled in the Hindu Kush in Afghanistan and hitch-hiked through the Khyber Pass. Eventually they reached Turkey, and got a bus 'up through Europe to Calais', Josie said, putting into five words a journey which must have taken many days and nights. 'Then we took a ferry to Dover.'

'And what was your first impression of Dover – apart from the cliffs?'

'I just remember thinking, "It's so wonderful, everyone speaks English!" I ended up at Victoria Station. I'd found somewhere to lodge in Ranelagh Grove behind Pimlico Road, through a contact I'd found on the journey.'

If she had met a different contact on the journey, she might have found lodgings in Hampstead or High Barnet. But luckily for the future Cameron House she landed firmly in the SW1/SW3 area of London. She offloaded her backpack onto the floor of her rented room, and went out to explore.

'London was nothing like I'd expected,' she told me. 'I expected it to be like *Coronation Street*.' Television soap opera exporters should bear in mind how influential their mises en scène can be to people in other countries. Expecting the cramped terracing of Salford, Josie was dazzled by the 'wondrous, gorgeous buildings steeped in history'.

She arrived in May, and was enchanted by everything. 'Train travel! The joy of sitting in a railway carriage, looking out at cottages with

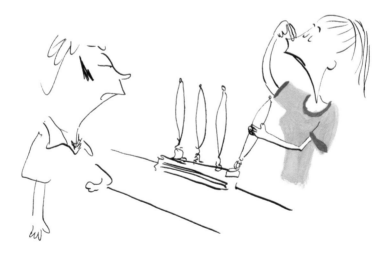

climbing roses! I had a friend who was a midwife in Wiltshire and I went to visit her. I remember the swans on the river, the blossom, the tea shops: everything looked soft and beautiful.'

Very soon she realised that she was going to run out of cash, fast. From an agency she got a job working behind the bar in a pub off Regent Street. 'That lasted two evenings. I hated the smell. But with those two evenings' wages I bought a tartan box-pleated skirt and a blue twinset from the Scotch House in Knightsbridge.'

So tartan had not lost its hold over her. It was deeply ingrained in her consciousness as synonymous with 'smart, well-brought-up and presentable' and it would look just right for interviews. She wore her newly acquired garments the very next day, for an interview to apply to do a TEFL (Teaching English as a Foreign Language) course. 'I got in – and then wore jeans for the actual course.' It was an intense month-long course: 'a lot of oral and written work, a lot of grammar – doing Latin at school had really helped'. In the evenings she worked as an usher at the Royal Festival Hall. For that, she had to buy a black dress, and here she gave me her views about black clothes.

'I hated black clothes. I even had to polish my navy shoes with black polish for the job. I've always been against teachers wearing black as I think it can have an intimidating effect on children. Black was banned in my first few years of teaching in New Zealand.

'I had always loved classical music,' Josie said, 'and you didn't get a great deal of live classical music in New Zealand – though I did once see Yehudi Menuhin perform in Dunedin. At the Festival Hall my list of favourite composers grew and grew. I had my own tip-up seat at the side of the concert hall.'

The TEFL qualification proved highly useful. She found jobs teaching English to people from Greece, Qatar, France and Italy, cycling all over London from one to another on an ancient green bicycle with only two stiff gears and an equally ancient cane basket attached to the handlebars. She had bought it with the Festival Hall earnings. At one point she was whisked away to Italy and then to the Scottish isles to be a governess. Not wanting to waste a moment, she also embarked on a photography course, and spent hours in the darkroom learning about colour-tone separation.

In 1979 she approached Gabbitas-Thring, the prestigious agency for teachers. (It has lost its Thring and is now called simply Gabbitas.) Hazel Chislett (who is still there over thirty years later, now Senior Advisor) took down her credentials. Through her, Josie applied for a job as a modern-day governess to the daughter of Lady Shaftesbury. Telling

Wow, it's NOTHING LiKe
Coronation St....
...not that there's
anything wrong with
Coronation St of course

me the story of this interview, Josie mentioned for the first time that she herself is dyslexic. Her pioneering work in helping other dyslexics was to be spurred on by her own experience. 'I was very nervous at the interview, and at the end I said, "Thank you, Lady Haymarket."' It was a typical dyslexic's mistake. In her mind she had confused Shaftesbury (Avenue) with Haymarket round the corner, where New Zealand House was. Luckily Lady Shaftesbury didn't hold it against her and she got the job, which took her through the summer.

With the further help of Gabbitas-Thring, Josie later went for an interview at the new Thomas's School in Cadogan Gardens. (We're getting close to the pivotal moment of her first being @adesk.) She was interviewed by Joanna Thomas and remembers being bowled over by her enormous English country sheepdog. For reasons, perhaps, of her

New Zealand accent ('pen' coming across to the English ear as 'pin'), Mrs Thomas declined to make her a class teacher, but took her on as a French and Latin teacher.

Very soon after this, David Thomas asked Josie, 'Have you by any chance got any spare time? There's this boy, Mark Somers. We want to take him but he's not up to scratch yet. Do you think you could give him some help?'

aargh! My pin

Chapter 3
Le Petit Grenier

I went to visit Rosemary Somers, the mother of the boy Mark whom Josie agreed to take on more than thirty years ago. She lives in Philbeach Gardens and had completely forgotten that I was coming.

'I thought you must be one of my pupils,' she said, answering the doorbell. One of her pupils? It turned out that she herself had been so inspired by the way in which Josie rescued her eight-year-old son from academic failure in 1980 that she decided to train as a teacher of dyslexics – and has now been one for almost three decades.

'Rescued' was not too strong a word for what happened, she assured me. Like so many parents groping our way through parenthood without an instruction manual, she and her husband (with the best will in the world) had sent Mark to what turned out to be the wrong school for him. 'The French Lycée. We were ardent Europeans.' It had seemed like a good idea that Mark would be steeped in French culture and brought up to be bilingual. But Mark did badly at school. 'He had to repeat the whole school year again – that French word *redoubler* – and he still did badly.' Far from being able to read and write in French and English, he could do neither in either. 'We knew he was bright,' Rosemary said, 'but he was unhappy at the Lycée, and sinking.'

They had a friend in Kent who was a remedial teacher and he gave Mark an unofficial assessment. His verdict was 'I think he might be dyslexic.' 'That was the first time I'd ever heard the word,' Rosemary told me. 'I mentioned it to the Lycée and they hadn't heard of it either. We withdrew him from the school immediately but had nowhere to send him.'

It so happened that at that very moment in 1979, David and Joanna Thomas were actively looking for eight-year-old boys for their new

WELCOME!

co-educational prep school in Cadogan Gardens. 'They were ahead of their time,' Rosemary said. 'They'd heard of dyslexia. They offered Mark a place on the condition that he spent at least a term in the attic being taught by Josie.'

A week or so later I met Mark Somers himself in the City, where he was working for Lloyds Bank in retail risk, intelligence and reporting, after getting a degree in Astrophysics at Oxford University followed by a PhD. (He has since left that job and is running his own business.)

'I remember going to meet Josie for the first time at her house in Chelsea. I was terrified.'

'We were so nervous, Rosemary said. 'I mean, what do you do as a parent with an eight-year-old who's illiterate in English? I dressed him up in his smartest clothes. Like all dyspraxics he tended to be quite dishevelled.' (Mark was dyspraxic as well as dyslexic – both, unfortunately, difficult words to spell.)

'But I wasn't terrified for long,' Mark said. 'I never got the feeling that Josie felt it was going to be a problem.'

In other words, Josie looked straight through the superficial problems of dyslexia and dyspraxia to the clever and high-achieving boy inside.

'She was marvellously creative, and made it fun,' said Rosemary, remembering that first term when Mark was with Josie in the attic, along with three other pupils. 'She used to cut out spelling words on banana shapes. Why that should make spellings memorable I have no idea, but it did.' ('Bananas were Mark's favourite fruit at the time,' Josie told me.)

'At the Lycée it was always so loud,' Mark said. 'I couldn't

concentrate. I remember the peace and quiet of the attic. I always had ideas much sooner than the ability to write them down. One thing I really struggled with was upper and lower case letters. The mix confused me. So Josie got me reading *The Beano*, which was all in capitals – picture stories. That got me started as a reader. I thought, "This doesn't feel like school, reading comics."'

Within a few terms, Mark was ready to go into the main school.

How, I asked him, did he later manage (as a dyslexic) to master and remember all the formulae you need for a science doctorate? He gave me an insight into the dyslexic's method for acquiring knowledge: 'You have to learn things in different ways. Things don't get absorbed simply by looking at a page. You have to have a story, a narrative about what's going on. When I was doing Physics at Oxford, a lot of people were trying to learn formulae off by heart. I couldn't remember formulae, and never tried – at least, not in the way of remembering letters and symbols. What I did remember and understand were the principles behind the formulae. That was probably more useful in the end than just remembering the symbols.'

Although dyslexia was hardly mentioned, let alone understood, in most British educational establishments in 1979, the word 'dyslexia' had in fact been coined almost a century beforehand. The first recorded use of the term was in 1887, in a monograph by the ophthalmologist Rudolf Berlin of Stuttgart. That monograph was written up in the *British Medical Journal* by Dr Pringle Morgan in 1896, at which point it was made clear to the British public that there was such a thing as 'congenital word-blindness'. The paper

described the case of a fourteen-year-old boy who had great difficulty reading but was otherwise extremely bright. But, for eighty long years after that, British children with the condition were still made to live in a world of terrifying enforced spelling tests and rapped knuckles for mistakes.

In 1978, a Roman Catholic nun called Sister Mary John, who had just retired from a long stint as the headmistress of the Sisters' School in Sidmouth and had no intention of retiring from education altogether, founded the Dyslexia Teaching Centre in the Maria Assumpta Convent in Kensington – where it is still thriving today, in the same building, which is now Heythrop College. The current director of the centre, Jo Petty, joined in 1984. 'Sister Mary John,' she told me, 'was always fascinated by highly intelligent children who seemingly couldn't master the technique of the written word' – and she and her staff were determined to help them. In her full nun's habit and headdress, Sister Mary John would preside over morning meetings, starting them off with the ringing of a bell.'

In this dawn of the age of recognising dyslexia and helping dyslexic children, the pioneers were unflagging. Sister Mary John worked her staff hard. 'She would ring us at eleven at night,' Jo recalls, 'and say, "You must go and see that boy called Jeremy in Kensal Green tomorrow. He badly needs help." We'd say, "But I can't, I'm busy at Norland Place tomorrow." And she would say, "No, dear you've got time to do both: off you go."'

Josie was very much at the forefront of this new movement and this new dawn. 'Josie was much talked about,' Jo Petty said. 'She was mentioned in the same breath as other luminaries in the world of dyslexia, such as Daphne Hamilton-Fairley.' Daphne Hamilton-Fairley founded the school for dyslexics and dyspraxics Fairley House in 1982, in memory of her husband Gordon Hamilton-Fairley, who had been killed by an IRA bomb in Campden Hill Square in 1975. Fairley House, too, is still going strong. These women were all bringing a longed-for answer to prayer for many parents, who had felt as if they were banging their heads against brick walls trying to get their children understood, accepted and respected by teachers in mainstream schools.

'We weren't even in at attic at first,' Josie told me, about her first few months @adesk. 'We were in a corridor outside the headmaster's office.' Josie described the desk lovingly and in detail. 'It was an old desk, studded with pen marks, and unbalanced: every single leg moved.

I painted it again and again, trying to fill in the holes – so it was impossible for pupils to resist digging their pencils into the paint and levering off little flakes. The desk had a deep inkwell at the back, and this brought back memories of the inkwells we used to have at Columba College: we used to collect daisies from the lawn and slip them into the inkwells and watch them drink up the blue ink, and the petals would magically change colour from white to blue.'

The desk became 'a famous thinking-point', Josie said: 'a place of wonderfully constructive learning'. But the longed-for peace and quiet tended to be short-lived: 'We'd just be in the middle of getting to grips with a challenging concept, when there'd be a throng of vigorous, happy children stampeding down the corridor. It wasn't conducive to studying.'

She had a word with the Thomases, asking them whether there

might be a quieter space in the building. They told her there was an attic room, but it was stuffed with furniture. 'So one Sunday,' Josie said, 'we hired a van and took all the furniture out.' At last Josie had her own room, 'and I painted it with four coats of paint, and it had a gorgeous large attic window, and we called it "Le Petit Grenier".'

She taught her small group of three or four children (Mark included) in the mornings. The atmosphere was vibrant, Josie said, and the little group basked in the joy of having their own secluded spot to work in. 'We did so much, and had such fun, and all the while the children were becoming unblocked: discovering that they could enjoy education, and that they could do it, could improve, could master the necessary skills.'

There were birds outside the attic window to watch and listen to. Josie purchased a gigantic cassette tape recorder and put on music by Mozart and Mendelssohn to inspire and soothe the children while they

did their sticking and glueing. 'They brought in their empty Weetabix packets and we stuck pages of *The Beano* onto the cardboard and the children highlighted the words they liked. We made games with words: we'd chop a collection of words up into two parts – such as "st/and" and the children would be asked to put them back together again. The aim was to take the fear out of learning, to see the joy. We made puppets out of old socks and did little plays; the children wrote poetry. I wanted them to enjoy words in every possible way.'

All the desks in the attic were pockmarked and rickety, but no one minded. 'You could practically make music with the ricketiness,' Josie said, 'especially during a spelling test.'

Talking of spelling tests, Josie recalled, 'I asked one boy to tell me his favourite food. "Spaghetti Bolognese," he said. "And can you spell that for me?" I asked him. "Oh," he said, "I think my favourite food's actually fish and chips."'

In the afternoons the Petit Grenier children joined the other Thomas's children for games and other activities. And Josie changed into jeans in the staff loo, and cycled to lectures at Goldsmiths College, University of London where she'd started another degree, in Psychology. Another degree course? 'I needed more education,' Josie explained to me. 'I longed for it, yearned for it. When I came to England I couldn't believe how much knowledge there was to take in. It was oozing from every doorway, every window, every pamphlet...there simply weren't enough hours in the day.'

The day came when the attic space was needed by the school for its new library. 'So I went and did the same thing in the basement of Garden House School in Sloane Gardens,' she told me. 'I had someone paint a beautiful jungle scene on the walls.' In the Garden House basement, pottery-making flourished. 'I loved teaching pottery,' Josie said, 'and Rabbi David Goldberg [OBE] and his wife Carol [parents of Rupert Goldberg] used to take the children's creations home and fire them. So kind!' Soon afterwards, that space was also commandeered, and Josie had to move on. It was as if Providence was goading her to find a place of her own.

'I was living in Eaton Terrace, in a tiny flat with alcoves and a bed that folded back into an elegant cupboard. My neighbour, Betsy [Dare], had a spare basement. I asked her, "Could I possibly borrow your basement?" She said yes: and here I set up my little group, mornings only, teaching eight children aged between five and eight. One of my pupils, called Saran Robinson, said, "This school needs a name: let's call it The Learning Tree."' So that was what it was called.

'The Cameron Learning Tree is a tutorial school,' said the first typed one-page prospectus, 'that caters for children who have specific learning difficulties, e.g. dyslexia, or who have not had teaching appropriate for entry into a conventional mainstream school. The children are enrolled for periods ranging from three to nine terms.' Josie's job was to get the children up to scratch academically and show them how to love learning, so they could be 'fed back' into a good mainstream school.

'Trying to get down to the bare bones of why the early Cameron Learning Tree was so successful and built up so quickly,' Josie said to me, 'I think it was partly because I am a notorious optimist, always seeing a cup half-full and never half-empty. I always saw the best in every child: I saw his or her uniqueness and amazing potential. I wouldn't countenance being defeated by a problem; I knew that if I explored all the creative ways of teaching and getting things across, every child could achieve the necessary literacy and numeracy skills, which they hadn't been able to achieve through the "normal route".'

There were moments of hilarity. 'I set the smoke alarm off most days,' Josie said (bringing back echoes of her toast-burning teens at Columba Girls' College). 'This was before the invention of the timed toaster. I had to pretend we were having a fire drill and get everyone out onto the street.' The house in Eaton Terrace was next-door to The Duke of Wellington pub (which the children called 'The Duke of Boots'), and it always seemed to happen that the 'fire drill' brought on by the burnt toast coincided with the pub's opening time. 'So the children would spill out onto the pavement, "in character", wearing their glove puppets and speaking in their glove puppets' voices, and the pub regulars would just be turning up for the first pint of the day. Quite a clash of different worlds.'

Then even Betsy required the group to move on. She was selling the house. Josie had to look for permanent digs to run the school in. 'I'd always gone to church at St Luke's, Chelsea,' she told me, 'and I approached the Rector, the Very Revd Derek Watson. He told me, "We have a new curate, Niall Weir: he's moved into one of our two little verger's cottages. If you like, you can rent the other one."'

The cottage was 31 St Luke's Street, just behind the great church of St Luke's – in which, incidentally, Charles Dickens was married to Catherine Hogarth in 1836. In this verger's cottage, The Learning Tree would be given space to extend its branches.

Chapter 4

Walter Woodbine in the Rose Garden

The new curate, the Revd Niall Weir, was taken by surprise one morning in 1982, when a woman he'd never met before introduced herself and told him she was starting a school in the tiny cottage opposite his.

'I hadn't been informed by the Rector about this,' Niall told me. 'I was quite far down the food chain.'

'How many pupils are you going to have?' he asked Josie.

'About twenty-four. Would you be happy to do an assembly for us?'

Three decades later, Niall is now the Rector of St Paul's Church, West Hackney. On his day off he came to St Luke's, Chelsea to revisit his past and tell me his memories of The Learning Tree. He's a walking advertisement for both the Church of England and Northern Ireland, from where he originally comes.

'That was typical of Josie,' he told me, as we walked through the churchyard towards the cottages at the back. 'She didn't know me from Adam. But she just had this trust.' Niall agreed to do an assembly; but

38

perfect

first the school had to be got ready. 'They were putting up shelves on the last night before the school opened,' Niall remembers.

'I made a lovely library in a double cupboard,' Josie told me. 'And I sewed curtains which looked like ladies' skirts.'

'You mean ruched blinds?'

'That's it.' (It was definitely the 1980s.)

Niall painted a picture of the free-spirited and slightly eccentric aura of St Luke's in those days. 'The Rector, Derek Watson, attracted positive, "can do" people – of whom Josie was one. It had quite a congregation. On my first Remembrance Sunday as curate I remember standing in the pulpit about to start my sermon and seeing [Field Marshal] Montgomery's brother in the front pew. You'd find Princess Margaret and John Betjeman turning up for services. Once, a rather scruffy and dishevelled old lady offered to help with the church's finances. We asked her whether she'd ever done anything like that before, and she said she'd been the Financial Controller of John Lewis for 25 years. The ideal person for the job! There was lots of inspired, eccentric stuff going on in the church, and The Learning Tree fitted into that.' Niall told me that his next job after leaving St Luke's was in Poplar in East London, 'which my bishop described as "a radical change of postcode".'

If you go to St Luke's Street, where the two cottages are, you'll see that they are joined to each other by a high brick archway. This is an echo of the old Gothic archway of St Luke's Boys' School, the parochial school originally founded in 1595 and rebuilt in 1824 at the same time as the building of St Luke's church. Josie liked knowing that there had been a school on the site for over 400 years.

In his speech at the laying of the foundation stone of St Luke's School in 1824, the Revd the Hon Gerald Wellesley (younger brother of the Duke of Wellington) made these lofty pronouncements about the virtues of parochial education: 'It makes useful those members of society who would otherwise be the destruction of it: it makes them good servants, good citizens and good men; above all it instructs them in that holy religion which reconciles them to their station in this present life, and bids them look forward with joy and hope to everlasting happiness in that which is to come.'

The parochial school – along with the East Window of the church – was destroyed by a bomb in World War II. After the war, the current church hall, the two cottages joined by a brick arch and six new houses, were built on the site. The six houses were sold to pay for all the rebuilding. And it was in one of the two cottages joined by an arch that Josie was to open her new little school.

The day arrived, the doors opened, and on a sunny morning in September 1982 the lively world of the relocated Learning Tree came into being. 'It was wonderful,' Josie told me. 'We had picnic lunches in the rose garden, the children played in the park, they went swimming at the Chelsea Baths…We became a fully fledged school, extending the day to 3.30pm. Lots of our pupils were dyslexic – children whose academic ability at the time didn't allow them easily to attain a place in a mainstream school. But these were some of the brightest children you could meet.'

It was time for Niall to take that promised assembly. It turned out to be the first of many. It was a warm day and Josie suggested that he could take the assembly out of doors, in the rose garden of the churchyard. Within seconds of starting, he discovered an important and slightly alarming fact: 'You can't just sit with 24 children and read to them from a book.' He sensed that their minds were wandering. Praying for inspiration, he spotted a group of dogs on their morning walk, sniffing and frolicking among the bushes.

'There was once a dog called, er, Walter Woodbine,' he began. 'Walter liked to play in St Luke's Gardens with his friends Charlie the Cocker Spaniel, Simon the Shaggy Dog and Gordon the Greyhound. Shall I tell you a story about Walter and his friends?'

The children assented. And this was the first Walter Woodbine story that Niall told to the Learning Tree children on that memorable morning, sitting on a bench in full clerical attire. I hope the reader will forgive this short interlude for (as it were) Assembly. As well as being a strong moral tale, Niall's impromptu story captures the atmosphere of the Chelsea streets and parks in which those first Learning Tree children grew up. Take yourself back to a sunny morning in St Luke's Gardens in 1982, where you are sitting cross-legged on the grass.

41

There was once a dog called Walter Woodbine ...

Walter and the new pup on the block

Don't you love the first day of the summer holidays, thought Walter Woodbine? It wakes you up with the promise of weeks of fun, of no homework, of going to bed later than usual and of all kinds of other delights.

Walter opened his eyes and stretched out in his straw dog-basket. He climbed out of the basket and waddled over to two dog bowls.

'Breakfast!' he said to himself, and he began happily slurping and munching, until both bowls were licked clean. Then he gave himself a good shake and set off towards St Luke's Church. That was the meeting place for the little group of Chelsea dogs of whom these stories tell. Simon the Shaggy Dog, Charlie the Cocker Spaniel and Gordon the Greyhound were waiting excitedly on the church steps.

'What's on the menu today?', the three dogs wanted to know.

Walter knew the answer to that question already – playing their favourite game of all: Wheelie-bin Wars.

The rules of Wheelie-bin Wars are simple. Pick any street you like and look for the same number of wheelie-bins as there are players of the game. Each player picks a bin and, on the count of three and a half, they leap up and grab the handle of the bin with their teeth, pull the bin to the ground and flip open the lid to see what treasures are in store.

You score 1 point for a cardboard box, 2 points for a plastic bottle, 3 for a food wrapper, 4 for one slipper or shoe, 5 for a pair and, should you be lucky and find a bone in your bin, then the score is an amazing 10 points. The dog who scores the most points is the winner of Wheelie-bin Wars.

And so, Walter and his three friends happily trotted off in search of some wheelie-bins. They were about to turn right into Flood Street, when a deeper than the average doggy voice called out from behind them, 'Good morning, Walter, Simon, Charlie and Gordon!'

The four dogs knew that deep voice well. It belonged to Arnold the Alsatian, a famous police dog. He lived at the Royal Hospital with the Chelsea Pensioners and, like them, was a much-loved feature on the Chelsea landscape.

Arnold was not alone. Standing at his side was a dog whom none of them had ever seen before.

'I'd like you to meet Peter the Poodle,' said Arnold. 'He's new to Chelsea, so why don't you four take him and look after him for the day?'

You didn't have to be a mindreader to know what Walter, Simon, Charlie and Gordon were thinking. There they were, seconds away from the first game of Wheelie-bin Wars of the summer holidays, and now they were lumbered with looking after this new pup on the block. Not happy at all.

'Hi, Peter,' said Walter, trying to sound as though he meant it. 'We've got some great games to play and we'd really love it if you joined us.'

'That's that, then,' said Arnold in a satisfied tone of voice. Then he trotted off for a well-earned snooze under one of the cherry trees in St Luke's Gardens.

'Well!' said Peter, who was very excited at meeting his new friends.

'Well,' replied Walter, who wasn't one bit excited at meeting Peter. Quite the opposite, in fact.

'Well!' said Peter again. 'I'll bet that you know some great games!'

'Indeed we do!' replied Walter, with an enthusiasm that hadn't been there two seconds ago. The other three dogs looked daggers at him. 'He's about to tell Peter about Wheelie-bin Wars!' they all thought in horror.

'Oh, wonderful!' chirped Peter. 'Do tell me your favourite one!'

4 points

5 points

1 point

3 points

10 points

'ello 'ello 'ello

'I'd be delighted to,' said Walter. This time, the others looked not only daggers at Walter, but swords as well. 'Don't even think of telling him about Wheelie-bin Wars,' was the silent message they sent out.

'Our favourite game is Hide and Seek,' Walter said. The other dogs looked on in disbelief. They'd never played Hide and Seek in all their born days. 'It's a great game – have you ever played it?' he asked Peter.

'No, never.' said Peter. 'Do tell me more!'

'With pleasure.' Walter went on. By now, the other dogs were wondering if Walter was going a bit funny with the summer sun.

'Hide and Seek is a simple game and it's great fun. To play it, you need a seeker and some hiders. The seeker closes his eyes and counts to twenty very slowly indeed, while the hiders run and hide. When the seeker gets to twenty, he opens his eyes and says "Here I come, ready or not!" and then he starts looking for the hiders and tries to find them.'

'Wow!' gushed Peter. 'Can we play it now?'

'Why not?' said Walter. 'Let's head back to St Luke's.'

The others now realised that there was method in Walter's madness. Without having to say a word to each other, they worked out for

one... two...
three... four...

themselves exactly what he was up to. Maybe you have as well?

'Right,' said Walter. 'Let's begin the game. OK – close your eyes and start counting,' he said, trying not to sound too much like he was issuing an order. And Peter did just as he'd been instructed. 'One, two, three...'

No sooner had Peter begun, than Walter gave Simon, Charlie and Gordon one of those 'follow me' looks. They sped along Sydney Street, over the Kings Road and right once again into Flood Street. When they turned the corner they stopped – all out of puff – and laughed to themselves. 'Peter will never find us here!' whooped Walter. 'Too right!' snorted Simon. 'We can get on with Wheelie-bin Wars just as we planned,' chuckled Charlie. 'And Peter the Pesky Poodle will be looking for us for hours and so he won't bother us one little bit,' giggled Gordon. And then they spotted four wheelie-bins half way down the street on the pavement, and the first battle of Wheelie-bin Wars of the summer commenced.

Meanwhile, back in St Luke's Gardens, Arnold the Alsatian woke up from his snooze. He made his way out of the gardens, only to be greeted by the sight of a poodle peering underneath the Rector's car. 'Why, hello, Peter!' he exclaimed. 'Whatever are you up to?'

'I'm having the time of my life, playing Hide and Seek with my new friends. I'm the seeker and I've counted to twenty and I'm looking everywhere for them. I'm not having a lot of luck, but then again, I've

50

never played before and so I expect that it will take me ages to find them. But it's all great fun, and I'm the luckiest dog alive.'

It took Arnold about half a second to figure out what was going on and what Walter and his gang were up to. And it took him another half a second to work out exactly what he was going to do about it.

'Since this is the first time you've ever played Hide and Seek, I'm going to give you a helping hand. You keep on looking out for the hiders here at St Luke's and I'll have a hunt a bit further afield.'

Off he bounded, as fast as his four old legs would carry him – right out of St Luke's Street, left into Chelsea Manor Street, then over King's Road and into Flood Street. There he saw, just as he knew he would, four green wheelie-bins with four behinds of various colours sticking out of them.

Arnold watched four tails wagging in the wind then gave a cough that could have been heard in Sloane Square. Suddenly, the tails stopped wagging – Walter, Simon, Charlie and Gordon would have known that cough anywhere and they knew that that cough meant business. Slowly but surely, they poked their heads out of their respective bins and, they could see that Arnold was not amused. Not amused at all.

'What exactly do you think you are doing?' growled Arnold.

There then followed a guilty silence, which was broken by Gordon saying, 'We're playing Wheelie-bin Wars, Arnold.'

'I can see that!' growled Arnold again. 'And what is it you are supposed to be doing?'

There was another guilty silence, which was broken this time by Simon. 'We're supposed to be playing Hide and Seek with Peter.'

'Indeed you are,' said Arnold. 'And that's what Peter thinks you are still doing, and what makes him think he's the luckiest dog in Chelsea.'

Arnold let that remark sink in before continuing, 'Now suppose he found out what you were really doing. How would that make him feel?'

Walter, Simon, Charlie and Gordon were good dogs at heart and when they thought about how Peter would feel if he knew what they

were really up to, they knew the answer straight away. And I'm sure that you know it too.

It was Walter who spoke. 'It would make him feel so sad and so upset, to find out that the dogs who he thought were his new friends had tricked him like we've just done.'

'Exactly!' said Arnold. 'And what you plan to do about it?'

This time it was Charlie's turn. 'I think it's time to go back to St Luke's and find Peter and try to be better friends to him.'

'Well said, Charlie,' replied Arnold. 'Go on then! What's keeping you?'

And with that, the dogs leapt out of their respective bins and headed back towards St Luke's in search of Peter the Poodle.

'Oh, there you are!' cried Peter, when they found him. 'I thought I'd *never find you – I'm really not much good at this game, am I? I must be a real disappointment to you all as a new friend!'*

If the dogs hadn't felt bad before, they certainly did now. How could they have treated Peter so badly? How would they have felt if someone had treated them like that when they were new pups on the block?

'We've been thinking,' said Walter, 'that Hide and Seek is a rotten game to play with a new friend – especially a new friend who's never played it before. But don't worry, we've got loads of other really good games to teach you – games that are much more fun too. Have you ever heard of Wheelie-bin Wars?'

'No, never,' replied Peter. 'It sounds tons of fun! Can we play it now?'

'Sure we can. It's the easiest game in the world to play. What you do is this. Pick any street you like...'

Arnold the Alsatian watched them from the Town Hall steps, feeling glad that Walter, Simon, Charlie and Gordon had taken Peter the new dog under their wing in the way that we all should do when we have a newcomer to look after.

And a great game of Wheelie-bin Wars was had by all. Peter won, too, which truly made that new dog's day. In fact, it was the first of many games of Wheelie-bin Wars that all five dogs would play together that summer.

Thus Walter Woodbine came into being, and he would become a legendary fictional dog. With Walter Woodbine as chief character, Niall told (and continued to tell, as a vicar in Poplar and then as Rector in West Hackney) countless spontaneous stories to children – tales that threw light on the human as well as the canine condition.

Chapter 5

A Haven – and Some Early Electronic Gadgets

The Very Reverend Derek Watson, the inspirational Rector of St Luke's under whom the storytelling curate Niall Weir worked in 1982, now lives in the Archdeaconry of Canterbury. He lives there not because he is the Archdeacon himself, but because he is married to the Archdeacon, The Venerable Sheila Watson – the first-ever female Archdeacon to enthrone an Archbishop of Canterbury, which she did in March 2013. Josie recalls the mesmerising Assemblies that Sheila took at Cameron House in the late eighties.

I spoke to Derek Watson on the telephone and could hear instantly by the way he spoke that he was the kind of enlightened person who would have said not 'why?' but 'why not?' when Josie suggested opening a school for 24 pupils in a verger's cottage. 'I tried to be as supportive as I could,' he said, 'because it seemed to me to be a very worthwhile idea, and Josie had enormous imagination and a persevering gift to carry it off. It felt good all along. I seem to remember that it built up and started to flourish from a very early stage. It was not one of those things that one had nervous nights about.'

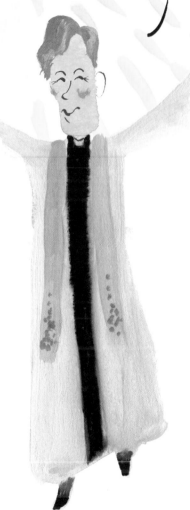

I asked about the dyslexic and 'learning support' aspect of the school: was it rare in those days for a school to cater for such needs? 'That was one of the exciting things,' Derek Watson said. 'Here was Josie bringing out into the open something that people were very naïve about. It was an imaginative and bold venture, and I think she deserves every bit of credit for carrying it off with such style.'

Derek Watson remembers his time as the Rector of St Luke's as 'one of the happiest bits of my life'. 'Josie's school was developing at the same time as a great deal of church building was going on: we raised over £1 million to develop the crypt. And while Josie was starting The Learning Tree, and Niall was living in the verger's cottage opposite, the church hall was being used as a nursery school called Ringrose – and that's still going strong.'

Working with Josie 'who doesn't have the word "no" in her vocabulary', Niall the curate gained a lot of confidence. 'I also got quite good at shinning up drainpipes, because Josie was forever locking herself out.' And all the while the Learning Tree children were also growing in confidence, basking in an atmosphere where they felt nurtured, valued and understood. These were children who had had a pretty hard time in their early years, clever but somehow failing in the mainstream system.

'Dyslexic children are often especially intelligent,' Josie said. 'But if they're not understood it can lead to changes of personality: they can become bitter, withdrawn – or "natural joker" types who feel compelled to play the clown. Dyslexics usually get from A to B by having to go from A to Z first and only then on to B.'

It was her and her staff's job to make this process as constructive and positive as possible. Bravely and against the grain of most educationalists of the time, Josie introduced an item into the school which was, at the

time, considered almost evil, and was certainly thought to be death to mental arithmetic and times-table learning: namely, the calculator.

'Calculators really were seen in those days as a death warrant,' Josie remembers. 'It was accepted wisdom that all children must learn times-tables by heart before being let loose on electronic gadgets. Well, I saw that calculators could be a gift to an intelligent dyslexic, who could be taught to estimate the answer to something and then to use the calculator to check that it was right. A case in point: Mark Somers, one of my first pupils in Le Petit Grenier, couldn't do the most basic times-tables when I taught him, and tells me he still can't remember seven times six. But he now has a PhD in Astrophysics. I found that the calculator was a concrete tool to support him, unlocking his potential and allowing him immediate access to the higher concepts of mathematics (which he, and many dyslexics, are more than capable of) – which would otherwise have been off-limits due to his lack of short-term memory skills.'

As with calculators, so with computers. These, too, were considered 'death to the human brain' by some. Josie sensed from the early days of personal computers how useful these could be to children who found handwriting a barrier to expressing themselves. They could be a tool to unlock and unblock dyslexic children's creative potential. Before computers were brought in, Josie introduced an electronic typewriter with a word-display facility. 'As part of my MPhil,' Josie said, 'I conducted a pilot study which proved that the use of such technology helped children to become able to transfer spellings into their long-term memory.' The advent of computers continued this progress. Early photographs of The Learning Tree show a 1980s big, chubby, grey computer which took up a whole table and had tangles of thick wires coming out of the back. 'In that tiny verger's cottage that computer took up a fairly large chunk of the percentage of desk space.'

Nowadays, of course, computers are widely used in school classrooms and it would be heresy to speak against them, just as it was a kind of heresy in those days to be in favour of them. Josie is a huge fan of the instant spell-check: 'It's fantastic and it spurs on success. The children don't have to be at the mercy of their ability, or lack of ability, to spell, and they can receive the expert help of an online dictionary: this is transformational. No longer is the dyslexic brain having to rely on memory alone for spelling, and nor should it be.'

Jane Emmett came to work with Josie as deputy head of The Learning Tree, and she was an integral part of its success. I visited her at Fulham Prep School, of which she is now the long-standing headmistress, and asked her about her memories of that time. 'It was

brilliant,' she said. (Jane had begun her teaching career in Buenos Aires, at a school run by the Misses Young, who no doubt deserve a whole book of their own.) 'It was a haven for children for whom it simply hadn't worked in other schools. Several of the parents were desperate when they came to us. They were at their wits' end about what to do.'

Such is the plight of parents who know, deep down, that their child is bright and talented, but have to see him or her consistently doing badly, coming bottom in the class, having had their confidence battered.

Just like Mark Somers before him, Sam Crosfield arrived at Josie's school as a refugee from the French Lycée. He was six years old

Andanoceantumbledbywith
aprivateboatformaxandhesaile
d o ff throughdaynadni g h t

and having extreme difficulty learning to read, and his traumatic school experience up to that moment had made him insular and insecure. 'The Lycée couldn't handle the situation at all,' he told me. 'They told my parents I was being disruptive, whereas I'm not that kind of person at all. It was just that there were 30 in a class, lined up in rows, and you were expected to be able to read from the age of five, which I couldn't. I became terrified of school. The thought of it made me physically sick.'

The label all too often given to children who had trouble learning to read in those days was 'backward'. 'My parents were really, really worried about me,' Sam said. That word hovered in the air around them.

His parents took him to an educational psychologist, who suggested that changing to a different way of learning might be a good idea. The psychologist had heard about The Learning Tree, and suggested that his family should visit it. They did, and Josie offered Sam a place. And Sam says, 32 years later, 'I can't imagine what my life would be like now if I hadn't been to The Learning Tree. Maybe I wouldn't have got an education if I hadn't been so fortunate.' That childhood change of fortune has made him, for life, a more appreciative person.

Sam's reading was definitely a record-breakingly hard nut to crack, as he told me himself. 'I was basically illiterate. I could only recognise a few letters. In my first year Josie and Jane had endless patience with me. They were so warm and encouraging, and gradually I started to relax. All the way through my first year, my parents were still worried. But then gradually things started to get better. There was no "Eureka" moment; I just began to feel more confident and happier, and the reading came with that.' He remembers The Learning Tree as 'comfortable, with intimate spaces and a reading corner', and that homeliness helped to break his mental block about school. Josie recalls creating the reading corner in a large double wardrobe, doors removed, bookshelves inserted top to bottom, with cosy cushions spread everywhere over the floor.

To this day Josie remembers Sam's natural kindness and sense of justice as a boy. 'I recall once,' she told me, 'birthday party invitations went out to all in the class except for one girl. Sam knocked on

my office door and told me about this, clearly furious at the injustice. I quietly asked him what he thought we should do about it and his reply was so touching. "We should go down there and do something about it!"'

Remembering the dynamic way in which she and her staff went down every possible avenue in order to find the right way to help each child to learn to read, Josie told me that the vital thing they needed to bear in mind was that all children were different, and that methods that worked well with one child might not work at all with another. They had to be sensitive and quick off the mark to notice what was and wasn't working.

For example, some of the children, who were very bright, found it impossible to concentrate with background noise in the room. 'I did some research on all this with the Baylor College of Medicine in Houston, Texas, where I studied for a whole summer,' Josie said. 'For the children who processed information differently, I procured headphones and microphones so that they received specific instructions from the teacher. It worked a treat with some of the children – but it was a disaster for those who didn't take to it. So I would only use this system with one or two children in the group who really needed it. Differentiation was crucial. One boy seemed very embarrassed about his headphones until we firmly planted Mickey Mouse stickers on the earpieces. Then he was sold on it.'

Josie had the idea, in the days before audio-books were in circulation, of reading books aloud onto a cassette tape, so the children could enjoy the books at home with their parents. 'I also gave them the choice of dictating their prep rather than writing it. This was always popular, and successful, too.'

Involving the parents was a key aspect of the Learning Tree method. 'At that time,' Josie said, 'the children had parents who were worried – some of them very worried – about their children. We devised graphs of the children's improvement – not just in academics, but expanding to behaviour and attitude, and this made it possible for teachers and parents to keep a close tab on how things were going. It meant that parents and staff were all in on the game of supporting, praising and encouraging any improvement on a child's "personal best". Success could be measured and enjoyed at home and at school by a unified and supportive team.'

Fiona Robertson came to teach at The Learning Tree and while she was there got engaged to Peter Cheese. She's now Fiona Cheese and lives in the country, where she keeps horses and alpacas. She told me some of her Learning Tree memories.

'It was gorgeous, so cosy, all freshly painted, everything just-so, a lovely place to work. It was more like being at home than at a school. Each child had such different needs. There were only 10 or 11 in the class, but I remember being amazed at how much work it was: you had to be extremely conscientious with each child. The children were so relieved to be in an environment where they were accepted.'

One of the pupils was driven to school every morning by a uniformed chauffeur. Another boy, Elliott, sometimes came to school in his father's white house-clearance van. On seeing Elliott arriving in the van, Fiona remembers the chauffeur-driven boy remarking, 'I wish

I could come to school in a white van. I'd love it.' A good example of inverted covetousness. And typical of Learning Tree children, who came out with such refreshing, wacky, honest remarks that sometimes the staff had to disappear promptly into the staff kitchen, unable to contain their laughter. Because they were such open children, 'they used to come out with comments that sent us into fits,' Jane Emmett said.

There was quite a variety of clientele at The Learning Tree, ranging from normal Chelsea fee-paying to multi-millionaire. One or two children came from such wealthy families that they arrived at school with not only a chauffeur but a bodyguard too. Ambassadors' sons and daughters came in bulletproof cars. One boy brought his two bodyguards with him for a sleepover with a friend from his class who invited him to stay at his family's country house.

A ring-bound copy of *The Learning Tree Review* survives from December 1982, onto the front cover of which is glued a photograph

of one boy giving a piggyback to another. Both have broad smiles revealing their large new-grown front teeth. 'At the beginning of term we transferred to a larger classroom,' Josie writes in the introduction (referring to the move to the verger's cottage). 'We outfitted it with handmade ruched curtains, apple-shaped cork noticeboards, apple-shaped blackboards and red easels, a fine marionette theatre and a pile of flat little cushions and large beanbags.'

Josie liked things to be apple-shaped – again, always fighting against the formality and off-putting atmosphere of so many of the world's classrooms. The magazine is full of stories, poems and drawings by Learning Tree children, all signed with first names – 'by Rupert', 'by

Chloe', 'by Juliette'. (Rupert went on to be a maker of fine furniture.)

We discover that this term the children have learned about the following: prehistoric times, Captain Cook, life in an Indian village, Marco Polo, Maps of the World, the whale, modern spacecraft and New Zealand sheep-farming. And never say that this was a magazine which repressed freedom of speech. At the end we get a signed petition:

> We demand a LONGER BREAK – and that's final.
>
> REASON:
>
> Ten minutes is FAR too short. Garden House School has MUCH longer than us and we think we NEED THE SAME or our brains might EXPLODE BECAUSE we are overworked and under rested!
>
> Signatures
>
> Rupert, Chloe, J.B. and JuJu.

The name for the Learning Tree's afternoon activities group? The Special Branch. This was a lively new arm of the school, and it offered the children the choice between Art, Adventure Playground and Topic.

> We have done a lot of painting this term in our Art Group. We use watercolour and poster paint. We have done a lot of pottery and Rabbi and Mrs Goldberg have kindly fired them in their kiln.

Josie signs off with three new ventures planned for the forthcoming term: swimming on Tuesday afternoons, piano and singing lessons on Thursday afternoons, and 'one or two lunches a week at which French will be spoken'.

Josie felt strongly about certain details, and she laid these out in a clear letter to members of staff who were joining the school:

INTERVIEWS WITH PARENTS:

All interviews must be conducted with grace, charm, discretion and tact. Please remember that parents of these particular children have cause to be more worried than the average parent, and that they, almost as much as the child, will need our help and understanding.

DISCIPLINE:

The discipline system is one based on encouragement rather than repression. If a child misbehaves, treat the situation as 'naturally' as possible and under no circumstances make a fool of him or her.

ARRIVAL TIME:

8.00. You are welcome to have coffee first, but please finish by 8.30. It creates a bad impression for parents to see tutors with early morning mugs of coffee in their hands.

DRESS:

Children with learning difficulties need to be in a bright and cheery environment. A tutor's dress is part of the environment. It is expected therefore that particular attention is paid to the care of clothes. Brightly coloured scarves and a variety of shawls are not expensive and can make all the difference between a cheerful appearance and a drab and boring one.

With these sound habits in place, The Learning Tree grew and thrived. Josie found that if a dyslexic child had an extra talent which he or she could perform, it provided an invaluable boost to his or her self-esteem. 'Whether it was ballet or tap, piano or trombone, singing or acting,

breakdancing or sport, it made an incredible difference. If a child didn't have an extra talent, I'd jolly well make it my business to invent one for them.' She advertised for a karate teacher. Why karate, I asked? 'I was so pro that wonderfully, exceptionally powerful discipline, which seemed so helpful for the discipline of the mind and body.'

'And I applied for the job,' said an extremely elegant woman called Lavender Ralston-Saul, whom I went to interview in her beautifully interior-designed London 'pad' with a kitchen in one corner, an office in another, a dining-room in another and a charming drawing-room in another. I asked her how she had come to apply for the job.

'I was a brown belt then,' she told me, 'at the age of 35, having started karate in my early thirties.'

'You started karate in your thirties?'

'Well, my husband had started doing karate classes, and I said "Maybe I'll come along to a class too", and he said, "I wouldn't, if I were you. It's getting rather complicated." So I said, "I'll come along next week, then." I was so entranced by being able to take up something new: to be a *student* as well as a mother! I had three children by then. The precision of karate suited me, and the striving for perfection, the pursuit of excellence…and that it could all be measured with coloured belts.'

Over the next 25 years Sensei Lavender would instil this enthusiasm and this pursuit of karate perfection into countless Learning Tree and Cameron House pupils, quite a few of whom achieved their black belts thanks to her teaching.

'Josie invited me for an interview in the cottage in St Luke's Street,' Lavender told me. 'I remember I was wearing a red skirt and my pearls. I rang the doorbell, and Josie opened the door. "Oh my goodness!" was her reaction. "You don't look at all as I expected you to look." They got on very well. 'Josie made me feel as if she was lucky to meet me, but I felt I was lucky to meet her,' Lavender said.

'Did you discuss the fact that many of the children you'd be teaching were dyslexic and dyspraxic?'

'We might have discussed dyslexia,' Lavender said. 'But the irony! Karate is so much more difficult for the dyslexic and dyspraxic child, because you have to have the correct arm or leg in front…you have to have good spatial awareness and co-ordination. But karate is probably especially *beneficial* for such children. I remember Josie rang me a month or so after I'd started. She was so happy: she'd noticed how

OH MY GOODNESS!
Lavender
Ralston-Saul

one boy who was doing karate with me had completely changed his attitude towards his academic work. She'd taken him for an interview at a senior school, and he'd talked about karate with such enthusiasm. She'd noticed that the spin-off from karate was improved academic achievement.'

Sam Farmar, who now makes documentary programmes for the BBC, was at The Learning Tree in the very early 1980s, aged six to eight. 'It was very friendly, encouraging and cosy,' he said. 'You weren't being barked at. I'd been at another nearby school up to then, but I think I might have been a bit dyslexic and that was perhaps why my parents moved me. Anyway, some of the boys who'd been in my class at my old school ended up with me at Eton, so I must have caught up.'

In the Special Branch's afternoon art club, Sam drew a picture of Father Christmas's back office, complete with chutes for letters and presents. His magnum opus, though, was 'a story which I decided was going to be the longest story in the world. I basically put into it every thought I'd ever had, together with every book I'd ever read and every film I'd ever seen. It ran to twelve pages.'

'What I aimed to do,' Josie said, 'was to accept every child exactly as he or she was, and then encourage them and gently, over time, empower them with the knowledge that there was a way to help them to acquire literary skills. They would always have an empathetic audience in our staff, and we provided them with incentives – some of which worked like rocket propulsion. Some of the children became prolific writers for their level, as a direct result.' Sam Farmar's magnum opus was a case in point.

John Vaughan, another pupil at The Learning Tree, thrived in the creative atmosphere. He remembers doing a picture of a lizard 'which the teachers liked so much they had it magnificently framed and hung on the wall. They took it with them when they moved.' (He carried on to do Art for A-Level.) He remembers excellent teaching from Jane Emmett: 'very caring, but also very firm, which you needed in a class where people came from lots of different backgrounds: you needed a firm hand to guide them.'

The boys' craze was for Garbage Pail stickers, which came inside packs of chewing gum: a parody, John explained, of Cabbage Patch

dolls, twisting the sweet dolls' names into 'Shaven Shaun' and 'Potty Scotty'. Along with a He-Man lunchbox, these were the current must-haves.

Clemmie Hambro (now Mrs Orlando Fraser) looks back on her time at The Learning Tree as a time of blissful deliverance from an unhappy time at her previous school, where she went up to the age of nine. 'The staff there said I had problems with learning, which I didn't at all. They said I would never get to boarding school, they made me do all these extra lessons...' All this had an adverse effect. Clemmie admits to having never been very good at maths – 'if my husband says "what's

73

five times five?", I start sweating,' she laughed, when I spoke to her – 'but I was never dyslexic, and from the day I first went to The Learning Tree I never struggled academically, actually.' She went on to develop a successful career as a travel and gardening writer.

'It was such a wonderful, caring, nurturing atmosphere,' Clemmie said, describing her overriding impressions of The Learning Tree. 'They took off all the pressure. It was a relaxing and fun place to be, and I was no longer in a state of tension the whole time.'

'Did the fact that you were in a less tense atmosphere actually help your schoolwork to improve?'

'Yes, it did,' she said. 'Suddenly it was a real treat to go to school every day. You could wear your own clothes, bring your own packed lunch. Josie was an amazing headmistress – she managed both to be informal and to command great respect – and I remember thinking it was amazing that we were allowed to call her Josie.'

Everything carried on happily in this haven of a school. But Josie was only renting the premises. Then one morning towards the end of 1985, the father of one of the boys at The Learning Tree had a quiet word with her. 'Look, I've found a building. It's in The Vale, and it's for sale. I've got a proposition. You want permanent digs for your school; I want a permanent school for my son. If you buy 51% of the building, I'll buy 49%, and you can buy me out in five or ten years at the price the building is worth at that time.'

'My instinct was instantly "Yes!"' Josie told me – 'and I hadn't even seen the place.' It turned out to be a charming redbrick house, full of food-lifts, which was already being run as a school, called The Vale. They were moving to new premises in Elvaston Place (where they are still going strong under the name of Eaton House The Vale). Determined to make this instinctive 'yes' a reality, Josie embarked

on the complicated house-buying process, with the conveyancing help of her fiancé's law firm Rowe & Moore.

Her fiancé? We must go back a few months to see how Josie's future husband had come into her life. When she'd first met him, he had kept his bicycle clips on throughout a whole dinner party. This had been precisely what attracted her, along with the fact that 'he could talk the hind legs off a donkey'.

Chapter 6
The Great Australia Hunt

The dinner party was in Islington, at the house of a friend who was an educational psychologist, married to a lawyer. Two of the guests arrived on their bikes: Josie, and Charles Ashcroft, a lawyer at the same law firm as the host. Quite a few of the guests were City lawyers in pinstriped suits; only one of them kept his bicycle clips on all evening.

'It was love at first sight,' Josie said. Charles Ashcroft was a brilliant man who had got such a high First in Greats at Christ Church, Oxford, that he had been invited to stay on to do research. But he was snapped up by the London law firm on the so-called 'milk round', when they came to scout for talent, and Oxford's loss was London's gain.

Cycling downhill from the dinner party together, they were kindred spirits already, and their relationship was to be one which made the most of cycling and walking in the English countryside. 'We used to get together with a group of friends at weekends, and do 20-mile walks,' Josie said. 'It was wonderful.'

But (as with Geoff all those years ago – who was now happily married to a woman from Toronto), Josie's longing for travel got the better of her. 'I had so much to *do*,' she told me. 'I broke it off:

I remember the moment so well, in a Fleet Street pub. I was determined to go to Inner Mongolia, and I did, with a group of eight people.'

For the whole of the summer of 1985, Josie cycled across China and Inner Mongolia. She and her co-travellers saw extraordinary things which Josie still thinks about often: a Buddhist monastery, to reach which they had to be hauled up a mountainside in a basket; the Mongolian steppes; friendly villagers; unfriendly ones with suspicious, wizened faces, who lived in huts; elderly women who had had their feet bound since babyhood; a lamb being slaughtered in their honour; and being given platefuls of the fatty, pungent meat which they washed down with green tea with melted butter in it.

To return to Beijing at the end of this long journey and see 'New Zealand steak' on a menu seemed like an astonishing leap back into the modern, cosmopolitan age. Josie flew back to Heathrow – and there, waiting for her in the arrivals hall, was Charles. 'I've put our engagement announcement in *The Times*,' he told her. 'It'll be in the paper tomorrow.'

And it was.

Meanwhile, the sluggish wheels of property-buying were chugging along, and 4 The Vale was making its way slowly but surely into Josie's 51% ownership.

'Wasn't it very expensive?' I asked Josie. 'There were so many noughts that you didn't take any notice after one or two.'

Her lack of prowess with numbers was probably a positive advantage at a time like that, when a more mathematically minded person might have been overcome by a violent bout of risk-aversion. But not Josie. 'I knew it was going to be baked beans and beanbag cushions for the next X number of years, but I didn't mind.'

'Our wedding date was the 5th of April 1986,' she told me. 'On the 4th, I exchanged on 4 The Vale. That was at 5pm. At 5.30 I had to be at the dress rehearsal for our wedding, at St Luke's. I just had time to get to Tatters to pick up the wedding dress (which had had to be taken in last minute) before it closed at 5.30. I got there with five minutes to spare. I was so anxious about the signing of the contract. One of Charles's colleagues and best man reassured me at the rehearsal, "Don't worry, it's all going to go through."'

On that very evening, Josie decided to name the school 'the *Cameron* Learning Tree – 'because, as I thought, "I won't be needing my maiden name again."'

So it was a breathless Wedding Eve; and there was an equally hair-raising moment on the wedding day itself. 'The person who gave me away was Sam Morton, the Judge. He came to collect me from my home in Smith Street in a vintage Rolls-Royce. But it was a Chelsea match day, and the King's Road was jammed solid.' After five minutes of going nowhere, Judge Morton (who was quite elderly) declared, 'I'm not going to have you being late for your wedding.' He emerged from the car, dressed in his morning suit, and stopped the traffic, holding up his white-gloved hand. 'It worked! We got to St Luke's only five minutes late.'

The honeymoon was spent in St Lucia (not a baked bean in sight), and then Josie came back to the last term at the verger's cottage. It was sad to leave; but everyone was excited: they were moving to new, larger premises in September. Josie had promised the pupils and their parents this, and was interviewing new pupils, so the numbers would double to 50 and more. There was extensive work to do on the building: those

food-lifts had to be turned into cupboards, for a start. The whole building needed to be gutted – electrics, plumbing, flooring – the lot. But there was a whole summer holiday to do that in.

Then the whole process hit the buffers. It was the first week of July. 'We had to "complete" by the 10th,' Josie said. 'The school holidays had started. And we suddenly discovered that two more signatures were urgently needed – the signatures of the two teenaged children of the vendors, who were part-owners of the building.'

But the whole family was nowhere to be found. Josie tried ringing them, but their secretary was sworn to silence. The family had asked not to be contacted under any circumstances. All Josie knew was that they had all gone off to Australia for the whole summer. Their solicitors tried to track them down, and gave up. Josie's solicitors tried to track them down, and, similarly, gave up.

'So we couldn't complete, and I couldn't open the school. My whole horizon was falling down the drain. We'd given up the verger's cottage. So we had literally nowhere to go – unless I was going to teach in the pews of the church, or in a rabbit hutch in Battersea Park. I'd undertaken to teach these children, and it had to be. If I didn't get those two signatures, all that goodwill would have been built up for nothing. But two high-powered solicitors' firms had given up!'

Sleepless, desperate and determined, Josie took the matter into her own hands. She decided to ring up every single hotel in Australia until she found the family. 'I fished out the international telephone directory,' she said, 'and started at the top [of Australia]. I rang every single four- or five-star hotel. The first five said they hadn't had the family staying there, so I fanned out from each of them, and so on, and on, scanning the whole country.'

oh... my .... God, Josie, the phone bill...

So worth it, darling

After eight hours on the telephone Josie's fingers (which were doing both the walking and the dialling) were getting tired, her ear was getting red, and her voice was hoarse from asking the same question over and over again. Then, at last, she hit the jackpot.

'I found the family at the last hotel before Ayers Rock.' Josie had even kept the scrap of paper on which she'd frantically scribbled the name of the hotel: 'Wallara Ranch, Central Australia'. 'The vendor was stunned, shocked and furious. But his children did fax me their signatures. I'd just reached them in time: they were about to go off in a camper van to Ayers Rock for three weeks, where they would have been completely uncontactable.'

With those two vital signatures, Josie could get the keys of 4 The Vale. The horizon suddenly opened up, wide and full of possibilities.

The summer of doing up the building was a blissfully happy one. 'It was so exciting,' Josie said, 'and our teams of builders were amazing.' They started at the top and the bottom of the six-floor building and met in the middle.

'They tore out all the lifts and made them into coat-hanging spaces. Every beautiful fireplace went away, which was terribly sad, but we needed every inch of space. All the doors had to be replaced in order to be made fireproof. I had windows put into the doors, to make everything lighter and brighter. I made colourful curtains and blinds to make it homely and child-friendly.'

Josie wanted the school to be full of joy and colour. 'Someone had told me that yellow was a "thinking" colour and green was the colour of calm. I commissioned stools to be made in the shape of daisies (which last to this day), and bookshelves in the shape of pirates and jolly book characters. From a bookshop I bought a lovely wooden tree which you could hang books from. The garden was concrete: we covered it with thick green soft padding, all over the ground and walls. We then painted hopscotch squares, chess and draughts boards and other games on the padding to provide lots of safe and fun activities.'

On the 17th of September 1986, the morning of the school's opening arrived. 'And on that morning,' Josie told me, 'I wrote off my car.'

'You did what?'

'Well, I'd bought the Revd Niall Weir's little VW Beetle a few months before. I woke up very bright and early and drove up the Fulham Road towards The Vale. [She and Charles were now living in Parson's Green.] And, you see, my mind was at school, though I was physically behind the wheel. We were bumper-to-bumper in a traffic

jam on Stamford Bridge going at 5mph at 6.45am, and someone suddenly came to a dramatic halt. I shunted into the car in front of me, and the one behind shunted into me, and so on. Six cars! After giving everyone my insurance details I pushed my car to the side of the road and just walked the rest of the way. I mean, what can you do?'

Quite. Josie arrived at Cameron House on the first morning of term to greet the children. An hour later, one of the parents arrived – Mrs Lorna Vaughan, whose son John had moved here from the verger's cottage, and whose daughter Blanche was also starting at the school. 'Mrs Vaughan walked in, went all the way up to the top floor, and came down again,' Josie told me. 'Then she said, "I don't know how you've done it; but you've managed to bring the atmosphere of The Learning Tree to this place."' From that moment, I knew the school was going to be a success.'

Chapter 7
The New Premises

The seven-year-old Blanche Vaughan (now a successful cookery writer) was at The Vale school in the summer term of 1986. As her brother John was starting at the newly opened Cameron Learning Tree (soon to be renamed Cameron House), her mother decided that Blanche should go there too. So Blanche had the odd experience of leaving 4 The Vale (The Vale School) for the summer holidays and returning to the same building in September to find it transformed. The way she described her arrival made it sound like the moment in *The Wizard of Oz* where the photography goes from the black and white of Kansas to the Technicolor of Oz.

'I remember being amazed: it seemed like a completely different place. More creative, more relaxed, a different attitude to teaching. No school uniform! [That was still to come, and it would never be a drab uniform.] Much less institutional-looking: it went from being one of those old-fashioned schooly schools to a much more colourful, attractive place, with coloured walls and coloured chairs. The whole place looked artistic, somehow. And we called the teachers by their first names, which we hadn't done at The Vale. We were allowed to bring our own packed lunches after all those years of school food in that

building. Suddenly there wasn't such a difference between the world of home and the world of school.'

Jane Emmett was a major figure in the lives of these early pupils at the new premises. 'She was warm, inspirational, one really respected her,' Blanche said. 'So often, schoolchildren spend their lives complaining about or mimicking their teachers. There was none of that with Jane. You felt a kind of parental respect for her.' One of the things many pupils remember is when Jane took the whole top year to her country house in Sussex for the weekend. This weekend visit became an annual tradition for the top year: the children played in the garden, sketched, went fishing, had barbecues, and, as Blanche put it, 'it felt like a real treat to be involved with her home life as you hardly ever were with teachers in those days.' Nowadays, before that kind of school outing could happen, a full and comprehensive Health and Safety assessment of the house would have to be carried out, and the result signed by every parent so they would know the risks. One hates to think what Health and Safety would object to today: the bats in the belfry, the lack of bars on the windows, the river running through the grounds or the lack of mobile phone coverage in this enchanting place.

When Glenys Dalgleish, an early Cameron House teacher who was brought up in New Zealand, came to talk to me, I was not baffled when she used the expression 'OE'. By now, I knew what it meant. It's a New-Zealander-who-longs-to-spread-her-wings word.

'I arrived in London in 1986, a teacher from the North Island,' she told me. 'I was 29 – I know, that was rather late to go on the OE.'

She was one of the new members of staff at the new Cameron House – which was called 'The Cameron Learning Tree' for its first few terms in The Vale. 'It had the most divine atmosphere,' she told me, 'wonderfully caring. I became the Year 5 teacher.'

Just like Fiona Cheese, Glenys Dalgleish recalled the huge amount of work she and all the other staff willingly and happily put in to tailor their teaching to each individual child. 'You couldn't just say to the whole class, "Here's a worksheet for you all to do." We were individualising programmes all the time.'

The children, she said, each had something unique to offer. They all had a sense of being accepted at this place, and therefore were happy in themselves. 'Some of them had come from schools where they'd been failing, where every day had been a struggle, and where they hadn't seen anything good about themselves. Josie was always looking for new approaches that could help them. She was a breath of fresh air.'

I asked Josie to give more examples of these 'new approaches'. Yoga was one of them, she said. 'Energy management was always an issue, so we evolved yoga classes, and exercises and stretches for blasts

91

of about four minutes every one and a quarter hours.' Again, this was an instinctive solution – common sense allowed to flourish and be put into practice to solve a problem, and it worked. Another approach: 'During art lessons,' Josie said, 'we developed classical music sequences of Mendelssohn's Violin Concerto, Jacqueline du Pré playing the Elgar Cello Concerto and Mozart and Satie piano music. The atmosphere was stunning; the children were so focussed and energised by the music. They progressed.'

It was not all plain sailing. There was one boy in the class, Glenys said, who couldn't laugh at himself at all and couldn't take any teasing. He got easily upset at little things. 'You know the way children laugh all the time in class, and he hated that. We wanted to say to him, "We're not laughing at you, we're laughing *with* you", but he just wouldn't take it. One day while we were playing football in Battersea Park he slipped and fell into the mud. We all held our breath. Then, suddenly – he laughed. And then we all fell about laughing. He'd got over that hurdle. We all helped him through that. Soon after that we started a folk-dancing club and he was the star of the show – so light on his feet. We wanted to bring things out that were there inside the children.'

Josie, Jane, Glenys, Douglas (Tate) and Dennis (Cox) – there were only two male teachers at the time: everyone was on first-name terms and this is still the case at Cameron House. Douglas was a teacher recommended to Josie by her friend Jane Emerson, who runs Emerson House. 'Douglas was known as the Pied Piper,' Jane Emerson told me. 'Children adored him and hung on his every word as if he were some kind of magician. He told them amazing stories – he was literary, an artist, amazing at capturing the children's interests and motivating them.' But after a week or so the Cameron House parents noticed that

their children in Douglas's class didn't seem to be learning any maths. It turned out that Douglas was teaching them absolutely masses, but no maths. 'I did feel slightly guilty,' Josie said. This situation (sadly, some of the children must have thought) only lasted a few weeks, until Josie had a word with Douglas, gently reminding him that a mathsless education was not acceptable. And Douglas mended his ways.

'That cloud had a silver lining,' Josie said, 'because after that bout of mathslessness we created a school shop in the corner of Douglas's classroom where the children could have endless practical maths lessons.'

In her stipulations about staff dress, Josie had written (in keeping with 1980s teaching etiquette) 'staff must not wear trousers' – forgetting

to bear in mind that some of the staff would be male. Douglas took pains to obey this command on the last day of term, when he came to school dressed in a kilt.

'I always liked to choose teachers who'd travelled a lot,' Josie said, 'people with breadth and depth and ideally another skill as well as their skill in the classroom' – and Glenys remembers (as well as a large British contingent) a Canadian, an Australian and a South African among her co-staff, as well as the well-travelled Jane Emmett who was deputy head. 'We had a very sound teaching background – all of us. We were very well trained. Which meant we weren't frightened to individualise a programme.' Glenys remembers another moment when she and Jane had to suppress their giggles. Glenys said to one of her girls, a French girl, Verushka, who was changing for swimming, 'Why are you only wearing half your bikini?' 'But in France,' the girl replied, 'we only wear ze bottoms.'

Getting thoughts and ideas from the brain on to paper is hard for dyslexics and dyspraxics. 'Children are so often measured on paper,' Glenys said, 'and these people don't always shine on paper.' She recalls a heartening moment when a girl in her class wrote her first-ever story on a computer. 'It was the longest thing she'd ever written, and it opened up a whole new world for her. From that day on she never stopped writing.' That girl, Josie said, went on to contribute regularly to the Cameron House news bulletins published every week.

Jane Emerson remembers recommending one of her pupils to Cameron House from Emerson House. 'This girl was in a very low state indeed – her parents were divorcing, her confidence was at rock-bottom. After a few months Josie invited me to see the school play – and there this girl was, standing on the stage, radiant and calm with her long tresses, playing one of the leading roles with great flair. I was so impressed that they'd brought this girl back from the brink.'

Nowadays when you think of Cameron House, you don't think of it as a special school for dyslexics.

'When did this shift take place?' I asked Josie.

As soon as the school moved to The Vale, Josie said, she started opening it out. Parents of dyslexic pupils wanted to send their non-dyslexic siblings to the school. 'At the verger's cottage, we had already been a melting-pot of dyslexics as well as articulate, fluent, English-speaking but foreign children who were very bright but needed to catch up with the English system. From 1986 on I was looking for any child who wanted a good education. Word got around quickly and our numbers rose rapidly.'

'It was while my son Josh was at the school,' said Veronica Bidwell (whose son Josh Ford was at the school from 1986 to 1989), 'that it transitioned from being a specialist school for dyslexics to a more traditional school – without losing any of its warmth.'

'When you've got a severely dyslexic child, you feel you're the only parent in the world whose child can't read or write,' Veronica told me. She explained what a profound relief it was to find Cameron House for her son. 'After years of having teachers who did not understand his difficulties and who would get cross or remove him from class, Josh now had teachers who encouraged and nurtured him. It was an oasis. You stopped worrying for a few years. You didn't have to go on feeling beside yourself because your child was struggling and having a miserable time at school.'

Josh learned to believe in himself and came out of Cameron House a confident person. 'All the children were encouraged to stand up and speak in public. I've kept close to my heart a certificate for his passing of the public-speaking exam,' Veronica told me. That was a proud moment. Josh now runs his own businesses.

'For me the school was Josie,' Veronica said. 'She was like a little elf, so tiny, so pretty, so sweet, but underneath that was the steely determination of a tough New Zealander.' Josie was determined to stick to her vision of what education should be, and was ready to go the extra mile for every boy and girl.

Perhaps it was time to start thinking about a school uniform. But it had to be a cheerful one, not a dreary one. Josie met the uniform department of Peter Jones and started discussions. The process took two years. 'They wanted us to have grey, black, or (worse still) bottle green, which I was brought up with in Dunedin,' Josie told me. 'I wanted something crisp and clear and jolly, something that

would identify the children as part of a wonderful community.'

'Did you consider doing without a uniform at all?'

'We were probably the only independent school in London not to have one. I decided we did need one, otherwise too much of the children's attention might go into what they were going to wear each day. But I wasn't going to settle for dreary colours. Eventually Peter Jones came up with cherry-red cardigans and jumpers and navy kilts or corduroy trousers. And white shirts.' (Josie admits to being 'very much a white-shirt girl.') 'And I did notice,' she said, 'that once the children had a uniform they did sit even more proudly and attentively in class.'

Round the edges of the Cameron House day, Josie was fitting in all kinds of other things. She was by then studying for an MPhil at the University of London, for which she sat up late into the night, writing

essays. And early in the mornings she went riding in Hyde Park. Not just trotting along, but doing vigorous things like overturning benches and jumping over them. Josie painted a picture for me of these mornings in the 1980s: 'It was beautiful, riding out through the dawn mist, with the Victorian lamps alight.'

But one day in 1988 she fell off her horse and cracked her spine. She went to a private hospital to have an operation, and came out with her leg paralysed. 'I could walk (just) on two sticks,' she told me. 'Jane Emmett was deputy head and did wonderfully well, keeping everything going. When parents came in to see me, I'd sit behind my large writing desk and hide the sticks. I didn't want anyone to know.'

'What on earth had gone wrong at the hospital?' I asked.

'The surgeon had put bolts and screws into my spine. But he'd put screws into a nerve by mistake. He hadn't mentioned to me that mine was only the fourth back he'd ever done. His superb reputation had been built on operating on knees.'

Josie went to another hospital and had a ten-hour operation done by the surgeon Henry Crock AO MD MS FRCS FRACS, who chipped away at the bone which had quickly grown around the invasive metal and up the length of the whole spine. He removed the bolts and screws. 'And as soon as that operation was over I started to feel better. It was such a relief. I needed months of rehab, but at least I was on the mend.'

Glenys Dalgleish remembers Josie suffering from appalling pain during this time, and bearing it stoically.

'Crock advised me,' Josie said, 'that I really mustn't have children after that operation. My body wouldn't be able to take it. But I went on to have three children – and I named my first son Henry, after him.'

When Josie became a mother she became Principal of the school

rather than a day-to-day headmistress, keeping the school's well-being at the heart of her concerns. She has employed a headmistress to work alongside her since.

From writing this book I have seen just how closely Josie is involved. She divides her time between Oxford (her main home) and London, where she has a mews house round the corner from the school, and where I (like the staff at Cameron House) have been treated to many delectable items from local patisseries Maison Blanc and Paul. She comes up to London in the middle of the week and seems to know all the pupils at the school, who greet her like a friend.

'Wonderful Jane Emmett,' as Hermance de Vos said to me. Her son Frederick van de Wyck was at the school at this time, and Hermance had (and still has) huge admiration and gratitude for what both Josie and Jane were doing. 'Jane noted that Frederick was doing well in arithmetic – and she moved him up to the top class in the school for maths lessons, so at the age of eight he was doing maths with eleven-year-olds. That really stretched him.'

Verity Bard, who was at the school at this time, said, 'The warmth and energy of the school filtered down from Josie and from Jane. They and the rest of the staff truly loved children. At some schools you feel that the staff don't actually like children very much, and you wonder quite how they got into this line of work. But that certainly wasn't the case at Cameron House. I was very dyslexic, but Jane and Josie sympathised and understood. They realised that dyslexics were just as bright as other people, but needed more attention in certain areas.' Verity went on to get good A-Levels and a university degree.

Like so many people I spoke to, Frederick's mother Hermance remembers the cheerfulness of the school's appearance, the brightly coloured walls and the friendly, well-trained teachers. 'Nice to make a school not like a prison,' she said, echoing Josie's views entirely. Why any school should ever bear any resemblance at all to a prison has always been a mystery to Josie, and from the moment she set up her classroom in Auckland, up to and including the present day, she has played her part in banishing this aura from the school world.

Chapter 8
'That Cathedral'

wow

Nothing could bring home more strongly the way in which the world's great buildings look *big* to a small boy than these words of Ed Donati, old boy of Cameron House, who went on to do very well at Eton: 'We used to have our carol services down the road in that cathedral.'

You can see how St Luke's Church, with its arching Gothic Revival buttresses, its imposing portico and its massive windows, would seem cathedral-sized to a child. This parish church of Chelsea has been a focal point for school services and concerts ever since Josie started The Learning Tree in the verger's cottage. She told me about a bit of improvising by the actors in the very first school carol concert in St Luke's. 'One of the three kings asked Mary, "Do you by any chance have a baby by the name of Jesus?" To which Mary promptly replied, "No, no, no!" So Joseph (played by a young boy called Jeremy) quickly came up with the words, "But, darling, you know we decided to call the baby Jesus."'

Mrs Lily Morton, the widow of the judge who held up the traffic on Josie's wedding day, has attended a great many Cameron House services in St Luke's over the years as a guest of Josie, and when I sat next to her at the school's spring service, she recalled another memorable Cameron House nativity play moment in 2012. 'Mary lifted baby Jesus (who was a doll wrapped up in a white blanket) out of his crib and started to settle him into her arms. Perhaps she had a new baby brother or sister of her own, because at that moment she rather roughly held baby Jesus up high to have a quick sniff of his nappy.'

Lily Morton, incidentally, was almost 102 at that spring service in 2013, and had driven herself to the church. The Rector had reserved a parking space for her, with two plastic bollards in her spot. She drove straight through the bollards, knocking them out of the way like skittles.

'We're very much a Christian school, in the broadest sense,' Josie told me when I asked her about the school's moral and religious compass, 'but we're fully accepting of all other religions, and discuss all religions openly. Everyone has a right to believe in what they believe in.'

There's no doubt, though, that going regularly to St Luke's has given the school a deeply Christian aura. Numerous old pupils I have spoken to remember inspiring moments in St Luke's Church, perhaps singing or playing a solo, or listening to music, or winning prizes, or singing hymns on the last day of the summer term.

'When children come into St Luke's Church for the first time,' the current Rector the Revd Prebendary Dr Brian Leathard said to me when I visited him at the church, 'they always stop and gasp. A lot of them have never been into any building with a ceiling as high as this. That sense of such a big open space, the light pouring in through the great window…it somehow transports them, takes them somewhere else.'

'A numinous experience for them?' I asked.

'Yes, certainly numinous. You want that magical first impression to stay with them, not to wear off on the second or third visit. But you also want the atmosphere of the church to be friendly and welcoming, not just awe-inspiring.'

In the heart of Chelsea, St Luke's is a church open to all, every day of the week. 'We have 300 to 500 people coming in every week,' the Revd Brian Leathard said, 'and that doesn't include the congregations at our services, it's just people popping in to have a rest, to sit down, to think and pray. Because we're so near the Royal Marsden and Royal Brompton hospitals, we have lots of people from there – both visitors and patients. We have people wheeling their drip stands across the road. And because those hospitals are prestigious national hospitals, we have people from all over the place. I ask, "Have you come far to visit your relatives at the hospital?" And they say, "Yes, from Aberdeen" or "Yes, from Kuwait."'

The church should be a place of hospitality and welcome, the Revd Brian Leathard believes, 'because it needs to imitate Jesus Christ. That's our role: to say, "It's not only what happens on Sunday that matters, but what happens every minute of every day that matters."'

In this spirit the church welcomes schools, and Cameron House is one of half a dozen schools that are welcomed into the church to hold services and concerts. The church can seat 1,100 when all the balconies are used, so it can even fit in the whole Chelsea Academy. I conveyed, as requested by Josie, her and the school's immense gratitude for the use of the church, and Brian said, 'We regard it as part of our mission to welcome people in. I know the relationship between us and Cameron House grew out of personal contacts between the school's founder Josie and my predecessor who went on to be the Dean of Salisbury, the Very Revd Derek Watson, and I'm delighted it has carried on.'

The church was built in 1824 – 'so it's Georgian, not Victorian,' Brian emphasised. 'The first incumbent was the Duke of Wellington's younger brother, and the church was definitely designed to be a big statement in favour of Establishment and national pride – rather going against the slightly arty and bucolic associations of Chelsea before that time – pleasure gardens and so on. But two incumbents later, from 1836 to 1860, the Rector was Charles Kingsley, whose son, also Charles Kingsley (who wrote *The Water Babies*) was his father's curate. And he of course was connected to the arts, so all the arty associations came back. And all that has lasted. The Rector of this church is always an ex-officio member of the Chelsea Arts Club – and that goes back to Charles Kingsley's time.'

All this tallies with Josie's feeling that Chelsea is a small, friendly, open, enlightened community where artists and musicians and men and women of the cloth can flourish together. I asked Brian whether he liked going to the Chelsea Arts Club and he said he loved it. 'Recently when I was there I met an artist called Richard Bagguley, and I loved his pictures. We invited him to hang some of his paintings in St Luke's, and we invited him to be our artist in residence in 2011. We commissioned him to do a painting of a contemporary St Luke.' Brian took me into the church and showed me the painting: a twenty-first-century doctor in a white coat with a stethoscope round his neck, holding a palette – patron saint of both artists and physicians.

Josie, who is similarly keen to say 'yes' rather than 'no' to new ideas, and to celebrate musicians as well as artists, has always taken care to bring musicians and artists into Cameron House who are not only professional and talented themselves, but also able to communicate their enthusiasm to the children and make everyone feel involved and that they have something to contribute. Such is the 'family feel' of the school that parents have always felt very much part of it, and have been happy – indeed, positively itching – to get involved.

One father at the school, Mike Batt LVO, the songwriter and composer who composed the music for (among many other things) *The Wombles*, used to come into the school to help with concerts in the 1990s. As his leaving gift to the school, he composed the music for a dramatisation of Edward Lear's poem *The Dong with the Luminous Nose*, and brought along the entire Royal Philharmonic Orchestra to play the music. This, of course, was the World Premiere of the show. It

took place in Baden Powell House and was a slick and well-rehearsed production. 'It was completely original,' remembers Letitia Redbond, who was a pupil at the school at the time and had a minor role in the production – as a bee. 'It felt like the school was part of something exciting and new. We had full costume – a real collaborative effort, with the parents' help.'

The school has always celebrated the talents of the people who come into its orbit. The talents of such parents are generously and completely voluntarily offered. Mark Knopfler OBE (singer and guitarist), father of two Cameron House girls, has with his company British Grove Recording Studios recorded school concerts and events. Of the school, he says, 'Cameron House is a dynamic and happy place and both our girls have thrived there.'

Another parent, Mrs Painter, who worked for Sotheby's, arranged for all the children in Year 1 to go to Sotheby's and sketch a Turner painting which had come up for sale for the first time in over 100 years. The outing to Sotheby's – one of several such outings in the early 1990s – was supervised by Philip Hook, Senior Director of Impressionist and Modern Art at Sotheby's, and the father of Louis and Sabine, who were at the school, thanks to hearing about it from their neighbours the van de Wycks. I visited Philip and his wife Angelique at their flat in Chelsea and they told me more about the first school outing to Sotheby's.

'The children were sweet, adorable,' Philip said. 'And deeply attentive. I gave them a short talk about the paintings in the sale. They sat spellbound. And at the end, when I said, "Have any of you got any questions you'd like to ask?", one particularly eager boy put his hand up and said, "Do the security boys carry guns?"' The day after the trip to Sotheby's, Philip told me, 'the children drew pictures of the paintings they'd seen and sent them to me as thank-you letters.'

Josie has always been keen that the children should be given hands-on experience of the real thing – be it a painting, an Elizabethan vessel, a sculpture or a castle – in order to grasp deeply what it is like and thus learn from it. Far from being classroom-bound and textbook-bound, the children have from the earliest days gone on school trips to widen their understanding and curiosity about the world. The traditional night aboard the *Golden Hinde* is a treat to which all Year 4 pupils look forward – and what better way, Josie feels, could there be to find out what it was really like to be one of Sir Francis Drake's crew?

Josie's initial excitement at arriving in London from New Zealand with the backpack on – and finding herself in a place where things to

learn, see and do were oozing out of every corner of the city – was something that from the very first she and her staff made it their mission to pass on to the children. If any parent or even grandparent has a story to tell, Josie invites him or her in. Angelique Hook told me that her mother, who had been in the Dutch Resistance in Limburg during World War II, came into the school to talk to the children about her experiences during that time. 'My mother loved talking to the children,' Angelique said, 'and the children were at her feet, riveted.'

Old girls and boys are invited back to talk about their lives and careers, and to show the children the infinite possibilities which are there for them in later life if they go out and look for them. One speaker had the children spellbound with his descriptions of life in Africa and Borneo. Out of his backpack he produced a genuine shrunken head – producing a gasp – followed by a machete – producing an even bigger gasp and luckily not producing the Health and Safety officers.

The school's nurturing atmosphere is the characteristic most vividly remembered by pupils. Such an aura is one of the benefits of not trying to expand, open satellite schools, or merge with other schools into a conglomerate. The school has maintained its family atmosphere and this, in a world of expansions into chains of schools, is something that parents and pupils value hugely.

When you go into the school, it feels like going into a house – which indeed it is. First, you walk past thirty or so children's scooters parked in two rows on the front step: a heartening sight. I was given a tour of the school towards the end of a summer term, and, after being escorted up the tartan staircase by the school secretary, I started with a chat with Lucie Moore, the headmistress, in her office with its miniature window-seat built into the bay window.

Some parents steer clear of small schools, fearing that the lack of space will hamper their child's progress. But what you lose from lack of space, I realised, you gain from the very fact of the small numbers. Every child in a small school feels valued and is properly known by the headmistress and her staff. 'I teach all the children once a week,' Lucie said to me. 'I really get to know them in this way, and it helps me to keep my finger on the pulse.'

A large part of Lucie's job is dealing with entrance to the school and exit from it. She keeps in close touch with the heads and admissions departments of all the top London and boarding schools, endeavouring to place each child in the school that will suit him or her best.

There was a knock on the door and the Head Boy, James Pentland, and the Head Girl, Juliana Beekenkamp, came to take me on a tour of the school. (School tours given by the Head Boy and Head Girl have been a feature of the school for many years. Sarah Nalle, who is

now working for a publishing house in New York, was Head Girl in 2001, along with Finian Frew as Head Boy, and she remembers giving tours every other Monday and this being a great privilege, along with counting up the house points at the end of each week.)

James was about to leave for Latymer and Juliana for St Paul's. Juliana said to me, about Cameron House, 'You just literally know everyone, which is really, really nice.' I was struck by the ingenious use

of space. Josie has affectionately described life in the school as like living in a submarine. 'On a school visit to the National Maritime Museum in Greenwich,' she said, 'the children were invited on board a full-scale model submarine to experience the conditions. "Don't worry," chirped one of the boys. "We already know how to move around in one."'

Wherever you look there are drawings and paintings by the children on the walls. We peeped into classrooms: classrooms in basements, classrooms in attics, classrooms tucked away around corners. Overhead projectors and interactive whiteboards were much in use, as well as banks of laptops and iPads. In one classroom, a history timeline was being studied and the children were being asked to put their fingers on their noses if they could remember the name 'The Wars of the Roses'.

James and Juliana pointed out more features, such as the Year 5 Feelings Box. 'If you're angry about something, you write your feelings down and put the piece of paper in the box, anonymously.' In one class *Lion King* scenery was being made. Each class, they explained, puts on a big play at least once a year, which is always performed in the very grand, modern Kensington and Chelsea Library Theatre with all the mod cons of lighting and sound. They pointed out the 'walk to school' chart, and the recycling bin in each classroom. They showed me that each classroom has a small library of its own. And 'from Year 5 onwards, we're allowed to use fountain pens.'

Very early on, Josie had the playground padded in order to make the fun accident-free, and she told me about an afternoon in 1988, when the children went into the playground 'in their red jumpers with the green padded playground as a background – very Christmassy in itself – and I hired a snow-making machine, turning the cogs myself from the balcony above to make the snow fall; and then Father Christmas arrived to greet the children: it made a cracking Christmas card.'

the Wars of the ~~Roses~~ Noses

Susannah Fitzherbert-Brockholes, who is now an environmental consultant advising on sustainability strategy for businesses and the Government, spoke to me in vivid colours, recalling her time at Cameron House in the early 1990s. As with many other pupils I spoke to, she began with an unfavourable comparison with life at her previous school.

'I'd hated my last school. The teachers were like dragons and one of them in particular had picked on me. We had to wear pinafores and it was all very strict. One of my cousins, Anthony Agnew, went to Cameron House, and that's how my parents heard about it. They weren't happy with my school, so they moved me over to Cameron House.' Then came the feeling of relief. 'The classes were so much smaller, and it was great that they were mixed. I had brothers and was used to hanging around with boys anyway; and my brothers later came to the school, two and four years younger than me.'

'If you shut your eyes and see yourself back at the school,' I asked Susannah, 'what do you see?'

'I see myself running up and down the stairs,' she said, 'bombing around the classrooms, playing in the playground, swapping stickers with all my friends behind the tree...I had an American friend who had gel-filled stickers, and those were like gold dust. We all had sticker albums, divided into themes – animal stickers were popular, especially furry animal stickers. We loved anything cute. And there was a big hologram-sticker phase.'

The other major memory for Susannah was being in school plays. 'In my last year we did *Snow White Goes West* at Baden Powell House. I was the evil queen, who was manageress of the Wild West saloon and really the local "madam". My mother, who's an amazing seamstress, made me three costumes: first as a Red Indian, then as a Spanish senorita

(I have a Venezuelan uncle who procured a kind of cycling vest with a frilly tutu, and my mother made a Spanish train to go on the back); and finally for the queen, a bright red leotard and a bright red lacy tiered skirt. My mother made costumes for lots of the other kids as well.'

It was always 'a big thing,' Susannah said, to be one of the main characters in the play. 'It definitely gave me a boost of confidence.'

I asked her whether she had ever been naughty and she remembered one incident. 'The kids who were left-handed were given sloped writing boards to put on their desks to make writing easier. I wasn't left-handed but I really wanted one of those writing boards – I thought it would be really cool to have one. So I pretended to be left-handed. It didn't last long: I was soon busted, but I was allowed to use a sloped writing board anyway, and I loved it.'

Sabine Hook, who went to the school in the 1980s, also remembers the drama productions. She is now a trained teacher, 'and as a teacher I can now see how ambitious those Cameron House productions were. We did amazing end-of-year musicals – *The Wind in the Willows* and *Annie*. I had quite minor parts – a tree, things like that – but I loved it. We'd spend hours of the summer term rehearsing, practising the dance sequences over and over again. Cameron House to this day always employs outside choreographers to enhance the children's acting talents.'

'The biggest compliment I can give Cameron House,' another old girl, Charlie Trébaud (née Wyler) said to me, 'is that if it had a secondary school or a university I'd have gone there in a second.' Using the horizontal back of her hand to represent the rungs of a ladder, she told me that going to the school in 1993 had helped her self-esteem and self-confidence to go from there (bottom rung) to there (top rung) by the time she left in 1998, as Head Girl.

Now she is herself a mother, married to a Frenchman, and they own a restaurant in Cannes called Mezzo di Pasta. Her story, once again was of not having been understood or nurtured by her previous school. 'I suffered from dyslexia and dyspraxia, and these learning difficulties just weren't recognised. At that time it was rare for a school even to

Susannah?

realise dyslexia was an issue and that something could be done about it.
You were just thought of as "a struggling child". The headmaster of my
previous school had said to my father, "You're just going to have to make
her work harder." My father, who's Dutch and had been educated in
the United States, just couldn't understand their attitude, and said,
"What the hell do they mean by calling my child stupid?" He walked
out and we never went back. We lived round the corner from Cameron
House, in Elm Park Road, and a neighbour who'd been there told us
about it.'

'Mainly,' Charlie said, 'Cameron House builds up your confidence. They never put children down, they'd never give up on you. The teachers were fantastic and they'd always try to find a solution. I remember Glenys [Dalgleish] taking so much trouble helping me with my fine-motor skills. The environment was never a controlling one, we were allowed to grow and be our own people, but it was structured and monitored. If you were good at something, they'd try to help you draw on that. I was good at drama and singing, so they drew on that to help me with my speech.'

After her eleven years at The Learning Tree and at Cameron House, Jane Emmett left, and went on to be the very successful headmistress of

Fulham Prep School. Josie needed someone to share the responsibility of running the school. She was now the mother of Lucy (born in 1991) and Henry (born in 1993), and she would go on to have a third child, Edward (born in 1996). Her marriage broke up in 1997, so these years were not easy, and intensely busy. She appointed Finola Stack to be the school's headmistress in 1994. For the next thirteen years Finola was headmistress, and numerous people I spoke to have fond memories of her inspiring presence.

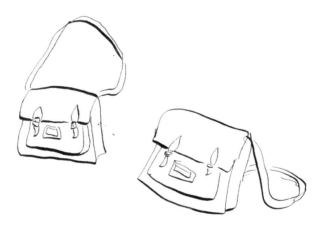

Chapter 9

Finola Stack, Karate and Paths for Life

On a hot August day, I met Finola Stack at the Bluebird Café, round the corner from Cameron House. The Bluebird is the nearest meeting place for mothers after morning drop-off, and many friendships have been forged there over the latte foam. Kathryn Green, the mother of three Cameron House children, told me that on the day when her eldest daughter Rachel (aged four) started at the school in 2003, she was feeling nervous and lost, having seen her little girl off to her first big school. She went for a consoling cup of coffee at the Bluebird – 'and there I met some other parents, and I made friends there and then with people who have become friends for life – I'm even working with one of them now.'

I asked Finola how she had heard about the school and how she came to be its headmistress in 1994. 'I'd been teaching in the building when it was The Vale School,' she told me, 'so I knew about the school. I'd met Josie at IAPS [Independent Association of Preparatory Schools] meetings a few times, and when I saw the job advertised, I rang her, and she suggested I apply.' So she did, and got the job, which she

found 'extremely fulfilling'. One of the many aspects of her job was to feed each pupil into the right one of the huge array of senior schools. 'You need to manage parents' expectations,' Finola said. 'My advice was always to try for three schools. But if those three were St Paul's, Godolphin and City of London, I said they'd better try for two others as back-ups.'

'I have incredibly happy memories of Cameron House,' she told me. 'There were fabulous children, fabulous families…really interesting, thoughtful children, who I know are going to grow up to become really good people.'

Thoughtful children – Finola's choice of that word tallied with what one of her ex-pupils, the above-mentioned Rachel Green (who went on to Godolphin and Latymer), said about Finola's ability to interact with

the children on a personal level. 'She was just the most amazing head teacher. She used to come into our class once a week and sit down and talk with us; she wanted to know what her pupils were thinking.' After a themed class assembly, 'Finola would pick up on something we'd said. She'd get us to think and talk about it.'

As Finola is now the headmistress of a girls-only school, I asked her how different it was to be the headmistress of a co-educational one. 'When you have boys and girls,' she said, 'you have to make sure you've got several teaching styles going on at once. In science lessons, for example, boys want to play with the equipment and see what happens; girls want more reassurance; they want to know "what am I dealing with here?" Boys are definitely more physical. I remember we had one boy who couldn't sit still, so we used to get him to take messages to other classrooms.' That subtle ploy made him feel useful and used up some of his copious energy.

Finola's three boys were at Cameron House while she was head-mistress – one year, all three of them were there – and this can't have been easy. 'It certainly meant they could never forget their homework,' Finola said.

Always there was (and perhaps still is, not just at this school but at almost every private pre-prep and prep school) the unstoppable tendency among parents to have their children tutored after school hours, in order to give them an edge over their rivals for getting in to the most sought-after senior schools. The prevalent culture of after-school tutoring is one of the great taboo subjects, even among parents, who often don't like to admit to each other that they're getting up to this kind of thing. Once word gets round, panic spreads, along with the feeling that one must keep up with the highly-tutored Joneses. 'Parents who don't have tutoring,' Finola said, 'feel they'd better, because everyone else is doing

it.' While she was at Cameron House, this trend was 'growing all over London.' Parents would ring up the teachers and ask them to come round after school to tutor their children. Josie and Finola put a stop to the staff taking on tutoring jobs for Cameron House pupils.

Just as Lucie Moore does now, Finola used to teach every class once a week: her subject was RE. I asked her how teachers manage not to have 'favourites' and 'least-favourites'. 'You have to be very careful,' she said. 'You would never want a child to feel that he or she was a favourite, and nor would you ever want a child to feel that he or she was not liked.'

I asked her about school trips. 'The children always loved the Science Museum,' she said. 'And the river trip to Chiswick for Geography. Kew Gardens were popular, too, and the National Gallery.'

Year 6 went sculling on the river near Putney Bridge and on residential trips to Juniper Hall Field Centre, and trips to Cornwall and Paris. 'It's good for children to go on these,' Finola said. 'Some of them have never spent a night away: it's good for their resilience, and for learning about themselves, and for learning to look after others.'

Ali Paterson (née Brumby), now a mother of three and the head of a nursery in Balham, taught the Cameron House Reception class and Class 2, and she remembers her time there as wonderfully busy, full-on and non-stop. 'It really was like a family because we all existed in one house. There was so much hustle and bustle as the children made their way up and down the staircases. And the children were so polite: I really was impressed by that. On my first day, a four-year-old boy came up to me and said, 'Excuse me, but would you mind tying my shoelace, please?' Good manners were definitely one of the virtues instilled in the children.

Coming from Whitby in Yorkshire, Ali was struck by the world of wealthy Chelsea in which the children grew up. She admired the tradition of the school day finishing at 2.30pm on Fridays so families could drive down to their country houses. She remembers observing one of Finola's RE lessons. The topic being discussed was the Ten Commandments, and Finola was explaining to the children that these were a set of rules. 'There are many rules which govern our lives,' Finola said. 'Now, can any of you think of some important rules we have to obey?'

A small hand shot up into the air. 'Yes?' said Finola.

'Don't ski off-piste.'

'Mmm, yes, that's a rule, I suppose. Any others?' Another hand shot up. 'Yes?'

'Don't use your mobile phone on Concorde.'

'And then,' Ali said, 'Finola gently steered the conversation towards more profound, Old Testament-style rules…'

The karate tradition at the school, which started in 1983, continued to grow. Josie took up karate and adored it, calling it a tonic. 'In the 1990s,' Josie said, 'I had canvassed parents, as I was considering establishing karate as part of the curriculum. I saw what an exceptionally powerful discipline it was, especially for our dyslexic pupils. After sending a questionnaire to parents I realised that this wasn't quite as popular an idea as I thought it would be, so I just extended the after-school sessions so they took place nearly every day, so that those who wished to could really thrive and excel.'

Not only did Finola encourage karate in the school, she took it up herself in a big way. 'I didn't actively promote karate,' she said, 'but perhaps it gained a higher profile because I was interested in it. We entered competitions and started winning.' Taught by the legendary Sensei Lavender Ralston-Saul, Finola gained her black belt in 2005, while she was headmistress of the school. 'Finola took up karate as a beginner,' Sensei Lavender told me, 'and she got her black belt with me. I thought it was an amazing testament that a headmistress could join a class as a beginner.'

During the 1990s there was a drive to make the school more competitive in the world of school sport generally. Rebecca Chubb (née Lewis) taught games at the school in the late 1990s (she was also a teaching assistant in Year 2), and remembers the change during those years from having class teachers taking games to having specialist games teachers. 'Up till then,' Josie said, 'it was normal for class teachers to help with sport. For instance I'd been teaching the BAGA [British Amateur Gymnastics Association] gymnastic awards for years, as I'd been a gymnast in my teens. And Rebecca was an excellent netball teacher among her many skills. But at this time we decided that the hiring of professional sports teachers would be a good step forward.' Rebecca remembers, 'Standards went up dramatically as a result. We started playing against other schools, getting out there and playing matches. It gave the children a broader physical education and it really helped them with their future schools, because they had sporting achievements and trophies to their names.'

Karate maintained its special place in the hearts of pupils and teachers alike – and some of the parents caught the bug too. A mother's karate group was started in one of the mother's kitchens, with Sensei Lavender as chief sensei. A few summers running, Finola and her three boys, and Josie and her three children, as well as some parents and their children, all went to King's Bruton School in Somerset to take part in Sensei Lavender's Gasshuku, a week of intense training and grading.

Everyone who was there remembers the combination of discipline and joy on the green lawns. 'You had to be immaculate with your katas and mae geris,' Josie recalls. 'Up before breakfast to train, and a great spirit of camaraderie.'

'The dominance of karate at the school was phenomenal,' an ex-mother of the school, Beth Colocci, said to me. Not a devotee of karate myself, and yet to be convinced, I must say Beth was an advertisement for it, being a karate addict herself and enviably lithe.

Beth's son Thomas was at the school from 2000 to 2005; her daughter Isabella, who was Head Girl, was there until 2007. At the time of our meeting Thomas had a place to read Chemistry at Oxford, but ended up going to Harvard, and Isabella was at St Paul's. 'By the time we started at Cameron House,' Beth said, 'everybody did karate,

including the headmistress. Sensei Lavender was a lovely teacher. What a wonderful thing karate is, to give these children focus and self-confidence. Isabella did it for her whole time there, she got up to brown belt.' Thomas, who went on to Sussex House for his later prep school years before St Paul's, came back to Cameron House to do karate with Sensei Lavender and the karate team after school; and through a chain of events involving another week-long Gasshuku which Thomas could not go on unless accompanied by a parent, Beth took up karate herself – 'and I'm still addicted. I train two or three times a week, for at least two hours, in Wimbledon; and Thomas does it too. We share it. There can't be too many boys who say they go home and punch their mother – and I punch him back! Thomas teaches me: young people are much better at learning things by rote than older people. Thomas can be shown something once and then four weeks later repeat it for you.'

I asked Beth more about the psychology of karate. 'It's much more about balance and strength than about losing weight and calories,' she said. 'It's more mental than physical. It's my head that hurts afterwards, not my body.' As for the addictive element, she said, 'It's very much a sport about constant self-improvement; in that way it has many similarities with ballet. You think you're good, and then you see someone else who's better, and you want to be better too. You have to face your fears – there's a lot of performing in front of other people. And doing that gives you self-confidence as you walk down the street.'

Finola, Beth said, would be in the karate class, with some students ahead of her and some behind. 'That showed a real willingness to learn. It's important for students to see their teachers learning. It turns the tables.'

As a headmistress, Beth said, Finola was 'lovely – always at the front door every morning, greeting every student by name.' (The same can be said of Lucie Moore, whose daily greeting of each arriving child is an essential element of her school day.) And academically, I asked, was the school stretching enough for clever children? 'It was flexible enough that they could feed up what a child needed. It certainly kept my daughter busy, and she gained a place at St Paul's.'

What's more, years later, Beth said, her daughter Isabella is still playing the bassoon to an advanced level, 'because she heard a presentation at Cameron House about "endangered instruments".'

Christina Floe, who was at the school for seven years in the 1990s, and was one of Sensei Lavender's karate pupils, said to me, 'I took karate up at the age of seven. It was a great way to do something fun together with my friends. We liked all the challenges and the gradings. Sensei Lavender was fantastic as a teacher, very good with small children, explaining things in a non-scary way. She could be fierce when it was required in an unruly class: I definitely remember sitting up

straighter. I got up to blue belt when I was there, and Sensei Lavender encouraged me to carry on with it – and I'm still going on.' (She's now in her twenties and is a black belt, 2nd dan.)

Aged 18, having left St Paul's, and having been accepted to read Psychology at Oxford, Christina went back to Cameron House in her gap year to help to teach karate. She remembers being struck, aged 18, with how small the school looked – this is perhaps a universal experience on revisiting one's childhood school. 'Children vary hugely in enthusiasm and natural ability,' she said, remembering her gap-year karate teaching. 'You get the lucky ones, who are both highly motivated and talented; you get some who are one or the other of those; and you get the ones who are really struggling. You don't know if they'll ever get there. But actually, the ones who stick at it and really persevere can end up among the best, even if they weren't as good earlier.'

All of these attributes of karate suit the school's aura – the way in which karate encourages perseverance, encourages you to have a go at things, helps with coordination, and promotes self-improvement in setting small personal goals. Josie showed me the first Cameron Learning Tree brochure, from 1980, which had printed in it the first school motto, which read: *'Good, Better, Best, never let it rest, till your Good gets Better, and your Better gets Best.'* A motto that could well be assigned to the goals of karate.

I spoke to Susie Stanford, another one of Sensei Lavender's star karate pupils, who was at Cameron House from 1988 to 1995 and is now working at Goldman Sachs. She remembers her time at the school as cloudlessly happy: 'I had an amazing time there: I loved it, and I'm still very close to a lot of people I was there with. I loved the way we learned there: it was quite a mature way to learn, with lots of discussing – the opposite of "learning by rote"; it was much more, "What do you think about this?" We learned to think for ourselves, to develop open-mindedness. I've noticed that something all my friends who were at Cameron House with me have in common is that we believe that other people's different opinions are worth listening to.'

Working as a sales trader at Goldman Sachs, Susie arrives at work at 6am every day, and works in a team of over thirty men and three women. This is where the confidence instilled by karate training comes in. 'Karate has helped me along the way so many times,' Susie said, 'in the confidence it gave me, and in the sense of self. It also taught me how you can be both *feminine* and *strong* at the same time, when you're working in a male environment: you don't have to become a "ladette" or anything, in order to flourish.'

I asked Susie how her karate life at Cameron House had started, and she said, 'I wanted to start because all the boys did it.' She never looked back; and she came under Sensei Lavender's spell. 'I thought she was so cool, because she was very English and feminine, but also a black belt. She made it an inclusive environment, even though there were lots of different levels. She liked to make you feel you were doing well and improving – and she was so passionate about karate and so brilliant, you wanted to be like her. She pulled rather than pushed: her standards were high but she was undyingly caring, and you wanted to do well.'

Just as Beth Colocci did, Susie admired Finola Stack's willingness to learn karate in the same classes as her pupils. 'She might be telling me off for something,' said Susie ' – and then an hour later we'd be doing karate in the same team. She'd gone from being my headmistress to my peer. I was giving her karate advice at the age of 10 – and I think it's a tribute to her as headmistress that she was willing to be taught by a 10-year-old.'

When Susie left and went on to St Paul's, she carried on with Sensei Lavender as her karate teacher, and achieved her black belt at the age of 16. When she applied to Goldman Sachs and put the karate achievements on her CV, she became well-known in the firm. People used to come up to her and say, "Oh, you're the girl with the karate black belt!"

Renata Cesar, who would become the first Chair of the Cameron House School Charitable Foundation, gave me a handful of random memories which had poured out from her children Chloe, Alexia and Michael, who had been at the school in the 1990s. Mulberry Walk, they remembered, was always known as 'Quiet Street' because the children had to be quiet there while walking back from swimming. In Assembly, with red hymn books, a favourite hymn was 'The King of Kings', and when the last verse of the last hymn ended, the youngest children in the school, not realising it had ended, would still be singing '...of Kings' when everyone else had stopped. Their little voices rang out on their own. The naughtiest thing Renata's children ever did was to throw water balloons out of the window on to the heads of waiting parents; also they made wet balls out of rolled-up loo paper and threw them onto the classroom ceiling, where they stuck.

There was (and still is) a Character Day once a year, when the children dress up as a character from a book they like. 'The children took it very seriously,' Renata said. 'The older ones were as into it as the younger ones. I remember my daughter Chloe saying, "I can't decide whether I should go as Voldemort or Mary Poppins."' Recalling this, Renata remembered the extraordinary word-of-mouth buzz about

Mulberry Walk, alias 'Quiet Street'

Harry Potter when the first book came out in 1997. 'My daughter Alexia said to me, "Mummy, you have to read this." Everyone was saying the same to everyone: "you have to read this."' Inspired by the book, her daughter Chloe went dressed as the Mirror of Erised (the mirror in which you see your deepest desire) – and, especially for Finola, who greeted all the dressed-up arrivers at the door, she made the reflection in her mirror say, 'Your three sons in the England football team.'

There was a special 'Cameron House clap', the Cesars recalled, which signalled that it was time to line up and go back to the classrooms at the end of break time. The school was full of 'good methods' like that, Renata said – for example, always sticking to the right when going up or down the stairs – sensible for a small building. And the fire practice regime was so well drilled into the children that years later, when her daughters were in their twenties and a fire alarm went off in Pizza Express, they instinctively stood up, were quiet, and looked around, as Cameron House had trained them to do.

The most amazing thing, Renata said, was the way in which 'Josie and Finola both had ways of setting children on their paths for life.' 'Josie met my son Michael a few years after he'd left the school and said to me, "You know, I know a boy who's a bit like Michael, who's a flying doctor in Africa." She put the idea into his head. He did go off to work in a clinic in Tanzania when he was 16. She'd somehow seen that in him. She had a deep instinct for what he was like and what he must be like now. And working in that clinic really made him sure he wanted to be a doctor.'

And Finola said, of Renata's daughter Alexia when she was 11, 'She's more sporty than she thinks she is.' 'She wasn't particularly sporty at Cameron House,' Renata told me, 'but now she's in the fencing team at Yale.' Josie showed me a striking photograph of Alexia sculling with

Cameron House on the Thames, looking focused, strong and inspired.

Emily Cotterell (née Berens) taught at the school during the 1990s, and verified another vivid Harry Potter memory told to me by Sarah Nalle. Sarah, who was at the school in the late 1990s and now works as an editorial assistant for the publishing house Simon & Schuster in New York, remembers 'our teacher Emily reading us the first Harry Potter book before it was famous. And we all fell in love with it: every single one of us in the class.' That was exactly what did happen, Emily confirmed. 'My great friend [the journalist] Helena de Bertodano interviewed J. K. Rowling before *Harry Potter and the Philosopher's Stone* came out, and she lent me her review copy. I remember casually discussing with her whether the children might enjoy it...and I read it to them in the week it was published and – well – they adored it. When it caused a sensation they were quite chuffed about being ahead of the game.'

The ethos of Cameron House 'formed my whole basis of teaching,' Emily Cotterell said, 'and I've taken the ethos with me. I've always chosen to teach in small schools.' (She is now deputy head of Badminton Junior School in Bristol, which has 120 children.) Cameron House was a school where the joy of reading was instilled into children from their first day. 'It was called "Time for ERIC",' Josie said: 'Everyone Reading in Class for fifteen minutes each day.' Ever since that magical Harry Potter moment, Emily has been strongly in favour of reading aloud to pupils. 'It gives them the opportunity to hear literature in a way they might not be able to cope with if they were reading to themselves. It introduces them to vocabulary beyond what they would be reading on their own.'

The mantra of education, Emily said, 'used to be that if a child didn't fit into a box, he or she was never going to make it in the academic field. Even now, you come across some people who believe that learning to spell is the be-all and end-all. Well, I've learned, through many years of teaching as well as having children of my own, that some children can spell and some children can't, and whether they can or can't is no reflection of how bright they are. Josie totally understood this. We had some children at Cameron House who had huge potential but just couldn't get it down on paper. It was just a matter of unlocking the potential. Josie was unafraid to encourage touch-typing, computers and spell-checkers if this would help to do the unlocking, which it often did.' Emily also remembers the wonderful work of the learning support teacher Glenys Dalgleish, who was 'fantastic' at diagnosing problems and at helping children out of them.

Another learning support teacher at the school was Heather Ouida, who now lives in New York City and has founded her own parenting website, Mommybites.com. Heather was also the teaching assistant for

Form 1, and she described the creative and supportive aura of the staffroom. 'The overarching thing I take away from Cameron House is that it was an incredible place to grow as a teacher. I was young – 25 – and many of the teachers were young, too, and we all grew as professionals together. We all supported each other and learned from each other. It wasn't a case of, "Well, this is how I teach, and if you don't like it, you can go your own way." We listened to each other and learned from each other and it was like being on a journey together.'

Schoolchildren, Heather said, notice if the teachers respect one another as teachers and as people; that sets the tone of respect in the school. 'Children are most open to learning when they feel relaxed and trust the teachers. They saw this group of women as genuinely supporting and trusting each other. They noticed that we'd leave the school together on a Friday evening and have dinner together. Our husbands became friends. We're still a close group now. I know that if I called any one of them and said, "I need you", they would get on a plane.'

Like Emily Cotterell, Heather appreciated the way Josie and Finola were ahead of their time in how children who needed learning support were viewed. 'It used to be a matter of, "Well, I'm afraid you're just going to find school hard". But we tried to see things from the child's point of view. Not "I'm so frustrated, I've taught this child a million times how to spell this word and she's still getting it wrong", but "what must it feel like to be that child, with the letters all floating in the air?"'

Being secure as a teacher is vital, Heather said. "If you're insecure as a teacher, children pick up on it and can make you question your own teaching even more. A secure teacher knows that it's not his or her teaching that's making it hard to get something across; it's that the child learns in a different way. As we know, the profile of these children is that they're very intelligent. We weren't afraid to ask each other for advice on good ways to teach children with different methods of learning.'

'Finola,' Heather said, 'was a mentor to me: we had staff meetings with her and private meetings once a week. I brainstormed with her and I could tell her anything. When she comes to New York City I still see her. She shaped the educator that I became.'

Suzanne Wyman, the mother of Katie, Jessie and Matilda Wyman, all of whom went to Cameron House in the 1990s and early 2000s, gave me an example of Finola's ability to spot and nurture a child's individual talent from an early age. When her eldest daughter Katie went along for her assessment aged four, she sat on her own working on the building blocks, fitting them together as they were meant to go. She was not working in a team, and a less far-sighted headmistress might have dismissed this little four-year-old as 'not a team player'. But Finola was drawn to this girl's quiet self-sufficiency, and she offered her a place. 'Finola picked up that Katie was self-sufficient,' Suzanne said, 'and when I see her now, I see that a lot of the things she does are self-taught. Finola spotted her strength: being individual, working in her own space, within her own imagination.'

Some of Katie's maths exam papers left a bit to be desired, from a purely academic point of view. 'They were sometimes handed in unfinished,' Suzanne told me 'with drawings of cartoon characters where the answers should have been. Finola awarded her the prize for "best doodler". At the time, she was working on this mad comic called "Supercow", about a cow who battled enemies who were lactose-intolerant, so Supercow could conquer them with milk from her teats. And now she's applying to study animation at university.'

From this we see the importance of nurturing rather than condemning a child's offbeat talent, which is a delicate thing, all too easily nipped in the bud. All of Suzanne's three girls were encouraged in this way at Cameron House, she told me. 'It was a real community there – really an extension of home. As a parent, you could slowly wean yourself off your children and they off you, as they went through the school.'

Dominique Kirby, whose children Chloe and Alister both went to the school, also treasures the memory of the way the school celebrated and encouraged rather than stamped out the children's eccentricities. Chloe was accepted, Dominique told me, by five or six other schools, 'but Cameron House was the one I wanted because it was small, and cosy, and about the children, not just about the grades.'

But how difficult was it to 'Get In'? All London independent-school parents know the sleepless nights spent worrying about getting into good schools. Melanie Young, whose son Jonathan was offered a place at the school aged four in 1998, remembers the feeling of elation on hearing the news. 'He came out of the assessment grinning from ear to ear. He'd had a great time.' But of course, that didn't mean he'd got in. You can have a lovely time at your assessment and still be rejected, such is the oversubscribed world of London private schools. 'When we heard he'd been accepted, it was like winning the lottery,' Melanie said. 'It was as if he'd been accepted into this private little club.' Her daughter Alexandra followed two years later.

'Finola was really kind and efficient and had the children's welfare truly at heart,' Melanie said. 'She didn't kowtow to parents, which I always admired. Sometimes she had to tell them things they didn't want to hear.'

Of the teachers, Melanie singled out Ali Brumby for particular praise. 'She was amazing – a real star. Jonathan was lucky enough to have her for two years. Jonathan is dyspraxic – trouble tying his shoelaces, things like that. Ali picked up on this and really helped him. At the end of the Reception year he won the Progress prize.' (Jonathan went on to Thomas's, then to St Paul's, and is now going to McGill University in Canada.) Alexandra also thrived at the school, becoming Head Girl in her final year. 'She's always been very "head-down" and focused,' Melanie said. 'She has a strong sense of responsibility. She had so many opportunities at Cameron House. At the age of eight she got through to the final of Junior Mastermind. Her specialist subject was 'Victorian architecture'. Finola gave her interview practice and really encouraged her in all that.'

A community of children; a community of staff; and now we turn our attention to the community of parents.

Chapter 10
Friends with small and capital 'F's

Picture this scene: a father at morning drop-off, early 1990s. With his daughter skipping upstairs ahead of him, he accompanies her up the four flights of stairs to her high-up classroom. On the way up the stairs, he kisses all the mothers he encounters who are on their way down. On the way back down, he kisses all the mothers he encounters who are on their way up.

The father was the interior designer David Bentheim, and the memories of those mornings still make him – and indeed, many of the mothers whose cheeks were pecked – smile, years later. David's daughter Amadea went on to St Paul's and then to Emmanuel College, Cambridge, to read History of Art. I spoke to David and he painted a picture for me of the friendliness of Cameron House, not only for children but for their parents too. 'We made so many friends there; we became godparents to their children and vice versa.'

David Bentheim stressed to me that Cameron House was 'social with a small "s", not a capital "S".' In other words, it was never cliquey, snooty or snobbish. 'There was a very varied mix of parents, and it was never too grand.' He mentioned two other schools (which shall remain nameless) at which the parents were 'rigorously smart',

dressing for school drop-off as if for a fashion show. Cameron House is more relaxed, he said. 'It also helps that it's a mixed-ability school: it stops it being overachieving, one of those places where children are made to feel left out if they're not doing well.' Such schools can make parents very wary of each other.

'We were invited by a South American mother to coffee on the very first day after dropping our children off,' David remembers. 'We became very involved quite quickly. Thomas Winterbottom's father ran the Chelsea Arts Club. First we had our class parents' dinner there; and later on there was a dinner for the parents of the whole lower school. There were about 120 children at the school, but, because of siblings, there were only about 90 families, and we really got to know each

other. People wanted to be friendly and hospitable. Always at the end of the summer term there was a drinks party for parents and the Year 6 leavers in someone's house and garden, and the leavers handed round the canapés.' This felt like a rite of passage for the leavers before they moved on to their senior schools.

'Did you and your daughter walk to school every morning?' I asked David Bentheim, expecting a description of a health-giving fifteen minutes with more pecks on cheeks from passing mothers. But his answer was 'No, I'm afraid not. We were exceptionally lazy and used to drive every day, doing a quick times-table test on the way. There was always a parking débâcle outside the school – but there weren't quite as many Chelsea tractors in those days.'

Dudley Winterbottom, the aforementioned father of Thomas, and also of Olga, both of whom went to Cameron House in the late 1980s, talked to me over lunch at the Chelsea Arts Club, which he has run for many years. He agreed with David Bentheim that the atmosphere of Cameron House was such that it inspired not only the children to be friends with each other, but the parents to be friends – and lifelong ones – with the parents. 'David and I used to go off for coffee after morning drop-off,' Dudley said. Rare – very rare – for fathers to do this kind of thing, I suggested, although mothers go off for coffee with each other as a matter of course.

Dudley remembered the Cameron House parents coming to supper at the Chelsea Arts Club. Again, he remembers that the conversation soared above the 'which school is yours trying for?' level. 'We got onto the subject of family backgrounds,' Dudley recalled, 'and we discovered that every single person there was the child or grandchild of someone who had been dispossessed at some time in their lives – in other words, the victim of some kind of revolution – and forced to emigrate. One was an Egyptian; one of them had a grandparent who had been on the Gold Rush; my mother was a refugee from Hitler...' That discovery brought home to him the international flavour of Chelsea in general and Cameron House in particular.

Parental partying is still a strong feature of the school. The end-of-year summer drinks party for parents has become an annual fixture in the calendar. In 2011, the Grassie family hosted it at their house in Holland Park, as a gift to the school. I visited Jorie Grassie, the mother of Lachlan, Alasdair, Gregor and Euan, all of whom have been at Cameron House before going on to Fettes, and asked her more.

'I just love that school so much that I'm happy to give a party like that,' Jorie said. Jorie's PA, Justine Loughrey, who was deeply involved in organising the party, described it to me: 'We had the weather, we had beautiful music, we had a beautifully decorated marquee, we had fun cocktails, canapés for the parents and a buffet for the children.' The party was supposed to last from 6 to 9 but it went on until after midnight. No one wanted to leave. The *pièce de résistance* was an ice-sculpture of the Cameron House crest, illuminated with LED lightbulbs.'

I asked Jorie to describe why the school inspired such generosity. She told me that her eldest son Lachlan (who is now at university in Texas) is dyslexic, and that the help he got at Cameron House was superb. 'He was never made to feel different. We moved to Hong Kong when our two younger sons were aged two and three; we left Hong Kong so the younger two could go to Cameron House: it meant that much to me. And the boys have kept in touch with so many of their friends.' When Lachlan was back in London in July 2013, he piped the Cameron House children into St Luke's Church before the annual summer prize-giving and concert. The sound and sight of that was so inspiring that it started a new tradition, Josie told me – and it couldn't but remind her of the McGlashan boys piping the Columba College girls into church in Dunedin in the early 1960s.

Jorie, too, has made many lifelong friends through the school. 'Our bond is having children at Cameron House – not necessarily in the same class.' As she scrolled down her phone list, countless names came up of great friends she said I must speak to.

One of these was Ana-Maria Rincon, a professional soprano specialising in the Baroque period. Her sons Oliver and Max were both at the school – and it was 'a golden time', she told me. She remembers being 'blown away' on her first visit to the school in 1997 by the way the whole class stood up when she and Finola walked into a classroom: 'It was old-fashioned politeness – the children were trained to acknowledge that an adult had come in. That clinched it for me, actually.'

Ana-Maria was one of the many deeply committed parents who

gave up their time to make sumptuous school events happen. 'My biggest job of all,' she told me, 'was as "social co-ordinator" for the most amazing Venetian Ball in 1999 at St Columba's Church, Knightsbridge, for parents and children.' Through her contacts in the Baroque music world, she managed to procure a Baroque orchestra to come and play at the ball – and asked a ballet dancer friend of hers to come into school beforehand and teach the children how to do Baroque dancing.

She also asked a baritone opera singer friend of hers to come and sing in a florid Venetian-Neapolitan way at the entrance to the party. This he willingly did, in full gondolier costume, standing behind (but it looked as if he was inside) a two-thirds life-size replica gondola made by some more parents. 'I also got Hayley Batt and Finian Frew to sing a Handel aria,' Ana-Maria said, 'dressed in Baroque costumes, accompanied by the orchestra.'

All the children had made and decorated their own Venetian masks in class to wear at the party. 'The joy of the school,' Ana-Maria said, 'was that everyone joined in and wanted to be part of it.'

More of the school's 'family' atmosphere was described to me by Lord Derby, whose three children, Henrietta, Edward and Oliver Stanley have all attended the school. Why did he and his wife (Lady Derby) choose the school? I asked him.

'My godson Malcolm Hamilton had been there. We wanted a very local school, and a co-educational one so that all our children could go there. As our country house is a long way away [Knowsley Park, near Liverpool], we knew they'd be doing an awful lot of travelling, so we wanted them to be able to walk to school. What the school lacks in space, it makes up for in the very fact that it is quite small.' The fact that it was not part of a 'chain' of schools also appealed. There are those school minibuses around London where the word 'Schools' is in the plural, but there's only one Cameron House. (Lucie Moore summed up the intimacy of a small school in this way: 'As headmistress of a small school, you know the name of everyone's dog and what colour scooter they've got.')

Hetty, who was deputy Head Girl at Cameron House and is now in her mid-teens at Wycombe Abbey, came down into the drawing-room of the Derbys' London house and joined in the conversation. She particularly remembered an excellent teacher called Ann Jordan.

Lord Derby described Ann: 'Of all of the teachers she probably pushed you rather harder than anyone else.'

Hetty said, 'Lilia was the assistant in Reception. We used to call her "lovely Lilia".' Lilia was in fact the runner-up in 2012 for the award for best teaching assistant in London and the South.

'Do you remember Lavender, the karate teacher?' I asked.

'Sensei Lavender!' exclaimed Lord Derby. 'Marvellous. About three strings of pearls...'

'And what crazes were going round the school when you were there?' I asked Hetty.

'For the girls it was Tamagotchis. We had them attached to the Cameron House rucksack. You had to wake them up, feed them and walk them. There was also a bit of a craze on that plastic spaghetti (called Scooby Doos) which you'd plait into patterns.'

I asked them about the many nationalities of the children at Cameron House, and Lord Derby said that was and still is a very international school, perhaps partly a function of the property prices in Chelsea. 'French families, Spanish, American, Canadian, Swedish... out of Hetty's final class of ten children, only two were English.' The pattern was more pronounced than usual in that class, but is evident every year. Lord Derby said how different this was from Ludgrove, which is 'an extraordinary microcosm of English aristocratic society'.

Josie had told me that the Derbys had invited the whole of Year 6 up to Knowsley for a term-time weekend. I asked Lord Derby about this.

'It was a girls' trip,' he said, 'as there happened to be no boys in that year. They came up in a minibus. They were picked up on Friday lunchtime – it was March, I remember, Mothering Sunday weekend, and they all picked masses of daffodils to bring back home to their mothers.'

It was an 'action-packed weekend' – Knowsley Park is a safari

park and the girls had a day of feeding the elephants and going on Knowsley's famous 'Aerial Extreme' walkway, before being given a life-saving training session in Knowsley's indoor pool on Saturday evening by a woman who worked at the local sports centre. 'The girls were all in their pyjamas. Half were rescuers, the other half were rescued.' On Sunday morning they were given a tour of the house, and then there was a big bonfire. All a far cry from London-weekend pursuits, and the daffodil-loaded girls came back home rosy-cheeked.

I spoke to the above-mentioned 'lovely Lilia', whose name is Lilia Beckett and who worked at the school for ten years from 1998, as a teaching assistant in the Reception class. She vividly remembers one boy, Freddy Berman, who was 'amazing at telling stories. We used to ask him to stand up in front of the class and tell us stories, which were often about castles and knights. We tried to bring out the best in everyone.' She also can't get out of her mind the time when she asked a tiny, quiet girl in Reception what a baby pig was called, and the girl replied, 'a twiglet'.

Lilia also recalled a moment of inspiration: little Jessica Wyman was distraught because she'd forgotten to bring anything in for 'show and tell', which that day had to be something beginning with the letter 'K'. 'Don't worry,' Lilia said to her. 'You're going to have the best show-and-tell ever. Now go upstairs and get your sister Katie out of her classroom and bring her down here.' Jessica producing her big sister Katie as a show-and-tell exhibit was greeted as a masterstroke by the rest of the class.

How to harness (but not exploit) the energy, generosity, and willingness to get involved, of parents whose children were and are at Cameron House? Two organisations were founded by Josie, one to enhance the lives of the pupils and the parents at the school, and one a charitable trust to help those unable to afford a private school education or who have come suddenly upon hard times.

The first of these organisations was the Friends of Cameron House, FoCH for short, which was founded in 1988. Its mission is to bring the school together in a range of events throughout the school year. When a child joins the school, FoCH arranges coffee at someone's house to welcome all the parents of new boys and girls.

I asked Lucie Moore about parental involvement in the school, and she said, 'We can do a fine job on our own, but we can do a superb job if we work together with the parents. Cameron House feels like a very special family: there's such a strong network. It's not always like that in London schools. London can be a lonely place.'

I spoke to Wendy Miller, the Chair of FoCH in the summer of 2011, and she said, 'I've been surprised by how many people have come forward saying they want to get involved. Some of the nannies, too. And I've never been involved in a place where the dads are so involved.' Book sales, cake sales, a barn dance in St Columba's Hall, Knightsbridge, the spring fair in Baden-Powell House, each one with a theme (Around the World in Eighty Days; the Olympics)...these events are brought into being through the energy of many parents and their willingness to give up their time.

Two mothers, Suzanne Wyman and Chair of FoCH Tricia Nalle, organised a 'Families helping Families' event in 2002. 'We organised it,' Tricia told me, 'in an effort to have the children and parents involved in doing something to help the British Red Cross in the wake of 9/11. We raised £20,000. It was a massive effort, but everyone had a great time for a good cause.' The FoCH sprang into action straight after the Boxing Day tsunami of 2004, and raised £22,000. One of the parents, Melanie Young, took the money raised to Sri Lanka herself and it was used for the rebuilding of schools and fishing boats.

In 2005 the school celebrated its Silver Jubilee with a concert in St Luke's Church. It was quite a coup to get music composed especially by Sir David Willcocks CBE MC and Mike Batt LVO, as well as Mark Knopfler OBE on guitar, all on the same programme. Mike and Mark were parents of pupils and ex-pupils, and Josie is the godmother to Sir David Willcocks's grandson Douglas; she asked Sir David whether he would compose a school song for Cameron House – which he did. The song is sung at all special services and gatherings each year. He

wrote parts for eight different instruments, including violin, cello, oboe and harp, tallying with the school's instrumentalists of the time.

The whole school was involved in the concert. The music staff – including the virtuoso Bulgarian violinist Ivo Stankov and the acclaimed soprano Vania Vatralova, who have since married – gave their all to create an evening of music and talent. The FoCH was very much involved in preparations. Jules Flory was the Chair of the committed group of mothers who helped to make it happen. She remembers it being hard work but rewarding, and she remembers the 'exceptional' contribution of James Thorpe, the head of music at the time, who rehearsed the children and inspired them to produce an amazing sound with both their voices and their instruments.

Well-wishing messages from other schools, congratulating Cameron

House on its first 25 years, poured in and were reproduced in the programme. Josie wrote in her letter of welcome to the concert, 'Whilst we have come a long way since we started in the attic in Cadogan Gardens, our founding principles remain as true today as they were in 1980. Through hard work and prayer and through the values of trust and faith, we aim for each child to experience the joys of learning and to find happiness and achievement in an atmosphere of creativity, energy, freedom and independence.'

The second organisation to be founded was the Cameron House School Charitable Foundation. Josie had the idea of starting a fund to help scholars who would not normally be able to afford private school fees

to attend the school. 'I had a two-hour meeting with Michael Alen-Buckley and Bill Bollinger,' she told me (both were fathers of children at the school), 'and in that short time they helped me to structure the whole way it would work. They knew what we should be aiming for, and they had ideas of the sort of people we should ask to be trustees. They said, if we [the school] would do the fundraising, they would match what we raised. They were so generous, of time, of spirit, of financial funding, and of their enthusiasm.'

A cabaret evening for parents and well-wishers was held in November 2006, involving an auction of prizes, all donated by parents. A week in Cape Town including flights; a catered dinner party for twenty; your child's portrait in oils; a weekend in Marrakech; a framed Rolling Stones gold record, donated by Bill Wyman; a week's skiing in Verbier; a week for eighteen in Sardinia; a yacht charter in Greece. The money raised on this evening, plus the matched money donated by the generous benefactors, kick-started the Cameron House Foundation into vigorous existence, and it has helped children to go to the school who would not otherwise have been able to. The first pupil to join under the scheme was a girl who went on to win a full scholarship to St Paul's Girls' School.

Josie remembers the moment when the girl's mother rang her to apply for a place for her daughter. 'I was sitting on top of a jeep in Kenya taking a picture of a warthog when my phone rang. It was this girl's mother, ringing me from the Chelsea Library where she'd just seen the Cameron House ad for scholars. I could have done with the mobile phone during the Great Australia Hunt! As soon as I spoke to her, I knew it was going to be a perfect match. The girl turned out to be a real scholar and a true credit to the school.'

But Josie – and other trustees – tell me it's not as easy as you might

Ring Ring

Twiglets

think to find children to take up these scholarship and bursary places. State primary schools are loath to part with their brightest children, and it's hard to know how to find these children and where to advertise the places. Word of mouth and advertisements in local papers have worked quite effectively. 'Once interest has been established,' Josie explained to me, 'it's also a difficult task, as any school with such a programme would tell you, to ascertain which candidates should be given a place. Financial need, motivation, potential and desire all need to be taken into account.' The fund has also now extended its remit to include a 'Horizon Fund' to help families currently at the school who have fallen on hard times in the recession or due to sudden personal misfortune and family bereavement.

Another splendid fund-raising dinner was held at the Bluebird in November 2013, at which almost £60,000 was raised for the Foundation. Nick Bonham, loyal Old Father of the school, presided over the auction side of the evening, inspiring high-spirited bidding from the guests with his charming, half-teasing auctioneering style, and the frequent taking-off and putting-back-on of his reading glasses. Enticing items were generously donated, ranging from prime tickets for a Chelsea football match to a box at the Albert Hall to see the Cirque du Soleil.

The school is always looking for children who would benefit from and make the most of the unique atmosphere and education the school has to offer. 'We're longing,' Josie said, 'to find parents who look in our direction, who really value education.'

I spoke to Michael and Gianni Alen-Buckley, the parents of Luke and Portia, who thrived at the school in the 1990s, and asked them more about what it was about Cameron House that inspired their generosity and love. (Gianni mentioned that they were 'everlasting friends' with the Bentheims, having met them while being parents at the school.) Michael modestly dropped into the conversation that 'we were involved in financing and getting the computer room up and running.' I pressed him and Gianni for more about this.

Gianni said, 'Finola had said to us – just a passing comment, really – "Gosh, it would be so fabulous if we had a computer room." I spoke to Michael, and he said, "Lets get the Bollingers and the LaGranges on board, and let's do it." The result was not only an ICT room, but an air-conditioned one.

'It was appropriate,' Gianni said. 'It was for love of Finola, for love of Josie; they had been fabulous to our children; this was a way of saying thank you and helping out.'

'The school was really open and inclusive,' Gianni said. 'We'd had a bit of a run-in with schools for our son. They hadn't realised he was very dyslexic, in spite of being good at verbal reasoning skills and maths. I went in [to his previous school] and saw him sitting on his own with his desk facing the wall. They said it was so that he wouldn't be distracted and distracting. But he was separated from the rest of the class, and that didn't feel right. We took him away. As soon as we walked into Cameron House it felt like coming home. They took him, and he flourished. They helped him massively with his confidence. They were literate in this whole thing of dyslexia; they didn't just think it was "a middle-class excuse for your stupid child", or whatever.' Luke has just done a Physics degree at Edinburgh University; Portia is at the Courtauld doing History of Art.

Angelique Hook used the same analogy – the 'coming home' one – when she described how her daughter Sabine came to the school in the late 1980s. 'She had been very unhappy at her previous school. She used to lie awake all night dreading going to school in the morning. A friend of ours had a child at Cameron House and said, "Why don't you go and have a look?" The moment I came into Cameron House I felt I'd come home. I think I wept!'

This culture of kindness, humanity, generosity and fun have been part of the school ever since it started and the Revd Niall Weir shinned up the drainpipes when Josie had locked herself out of the verger's cottage. As Philip Hook said, 'You feel tender towards a place where your children have been happy.'

Chapter 11
Lucie Moore, Zing and Moving Forward

'Josie set up this wonderful atmosphere, this beautiful learning environment,' Lucie Moore said to me, when I visited her in her office for the second time, in the middle of her long working day. 'That is the heart and soul of the school, the constant. As headmistress, my aim is to take the school forward. I want to be at the cutting edge of new initiatives and new ideas to take us into the future, without losing sight of the history of the school and without changing its values or ethos.'

Energy zinged from Lucie as she spoke. I could feel it bouncing off the walls. I could feel her energising me – and I was feeling particularly sluggish that day. It explains some of the school's 'buzz': if you have a headmistress who loves her job and always smiles and is full of zest, this has a trickle-down effect. Lucie cycles to school every morning (unless it's pouring) along the river from Chiswick (seven miles), arriving at about 7am, 'and I try to leave by 7pm in the evening.'

Her husband is a finance director, and 'both of us,' she said, 'are very sporty.' Every Monday evening (after the staff meeting) Lucie plays netball in a league. 'That certainly wakes me up. We play out of doors, even on winter evenings. And you can't bail out, because you're part of a team. I love it. It de-stresses.' Far from tiring her, this exercise seems to give her yet more energy.

'One of my strengths is that I'm super-organised,' she said. 'That's the Virgo in me! I don't think you could do this job if you were a little bit ditzy.'

You might think it would be less demanding to be the headmistress or headmaster of a small school than of a big one. But, talking to Lucie, I decided that it's just as demanding, if not more so, in a small school. If you've ever been shown round an enormous school where the headmaster has a grand office with a large mahogany desk and sofas and is rarely seen, and is certainly not known personally, by the majority of pupils, you'll know what I mean. On show-round day, he or she comes into the hall and gives a rousing speech and then vanishes again. In a big school, the headmaster or headmistress can hide away behind a mountain of bureaucracy, delegating all the daily tasks to his or her underlings. Lucie does no such thing, nor would she want to.

Bureaucracy does intrude, mainly in the form of the absolute necessity to keep abreast of new Health and Safety legislation. 'You have to get it spot-on,' Lucie said. 'That's one of the main things that has changed in the job, in the last 30 years. No one sends you documents about all that kind of thing; you're just meant to know about it.' Lucie finds it very helpful indeed to go to IAPS meetings – 'I'm actually on the committee with Finola Stack,' she told me. 'It's good to talk to other heads and share our knowledge and ideas. I also

thank you dear,
I'm here to see
the headmistress.
I'll see myself up

meet with a group called West London Heads. We all help each other. I see other prep school heads as allies.'

'When I started the school decades ago,' Josie told me, 'I was headmistress, Health and Safety officer, financial controller, HR [Human Resources] adviser, part-time secretary, teacher, and handyman all rolled into one. I regularly put on my Marigolds for urgent plumbing jobs. I became quite good at plumbing, an expert at taking U-bends out. On one occasion I was expecting a prospective parent to visit, and I'd put my Marigolds on to unblock a sink in the art room. The doorbell rang and I opened the door, in rubber gloves, to a rather haughty mother, who whizzed right past me on her way up to the head's office, saying, "I've come to see the headmistress."

I peeled off my gloves and chased her up the stairs as fast as I could. Her child started the following term, so she obviously can't have been too put off by the multi-tasking headmistress.'

Nowadays, the school has access to a wide range of professionals whose working lives are devoted to keeping abreast of the constantly changing requirements. 'We have two HR experts, a dozen different legal and financial advisors, a full-time bookkeeper on site, Health and Safety officers, fire-risk assessors, electricity safety checkers, as well as a merry band of cleaners who wear the Marigolds. We go to IAPS [Independent Association of Preparatory Schools], ISBA [Independent Schools' Bursars Association] meetings, and AGBIS [Association of Governing Bodies of Independent Schools] meetings: there's more to running a school these days than I would have dreamed of in the 1980s.'

Josie hugely admires Lucie's 'zip and zing', which percolates through the whole school and through all those involved with it. 'She's got her finger on the pulse at every level, which is crucial. She will always travel the extra mile to achieve the best result for a child. For example, she'll visit a school to which a child has applied, even if it is out of London or even abroad, so she can see for herself whether that child is well-matched.'

Lucie keeps her eye on both the big picture and the small picture: she aims to make the school better than ever and to help shape its future, while being fully in touch with every pupil and member of staff, every day. 'What I like about a small school,' she said, 'is that you're getting your hands dirty at every level. At a bigger school you can just be a figurehead, sitting in an office, dealing with angry parents and inspectors.'

Lucie also teaches every class once a week, and this is one of

the ways in which she gets to know every pupil. One of the many things she was going to do on the afternoon when I saw her was mark a pile of books from a lesson she'd taken that morning. She's constantly delighted by the affection that the children give – 'Children are amazing,' she said, 'full of love. Sometimes I'm feeling slightly stressed and one of the children will come up to me and say, "Can I show you the story I've written?" – and I think, "Wow! This is the best job ever. I mean, what a privilege!"' Lucie and her husband sometimes join Cameron House families going on the annual school ski trip, a highlight of the winter term.

Her job goes beyond caring for the children, she told me. 'The parents feel the connection with the school so strongly that they'll come and chat to me about anything. They come in to laugh and cry, to share something wonderful or to pour their heart out. As a headmistress you've got genuinely to care and genuinely to be interested. You can't fake that kind of thing. You shouldn't do this job unless you're really

interested in people.' Which Lucie is. She knows how bewildering the decisions and turning points of parenthood can be. 'Bringing up children has no handbook. Parents can make mistakes, even if they're on their fifth child.' She's touched by how appreciative the parents are of the school. 'We have the most gorgeous parents. People take the time to write lovely messages of appreciation. After the swimming gala last week I received cards, emails, lovely comments.'

One of Lucie's remits, she told me, has been to make the school fully co-educational to the age of 11. In the past, boys often tended to peel off at the age of seven or eight to go to prep schools – Ludgrove, the Dragon and Summer Fields, to name a few – which would keep them till 13, which was understandable; but now, Lucie says, with so many more boys' and co-educational senior schools taking pupils at 11+, it can work perfectly for a boy to stay at Cameron House till the end of Year 6. If he does intend to go on to a 13+ senior school such as Eton, Westminster or Winchester, there are schools where he can go for two years to prepare for Common Entrance. 'The work is still in progress,' Lucie said. The percentage at the moment is in the low sixties for girls and in the high forties for boys. 'But showing families round we're clear on the fact that we're not a school that prepares boys for the 7+ or the 8+.'

Staying till the end of Year 6 means that the boys get to be 'big fish', which is important, Lucie feels, for building up their confidence before they go on to a larger school. Also she's fervently in favour of the co-educational environment, believing it to be educationally, as well as socially, good for both boys and girls. 'Boys teach girls to lighten up, to dare to make mistakes; girls teach boys the value of focus and sitting still and studying.'

Many parents I spoke to felt the same about co-education. It's one of the things which attracts them to the school – especially if they have children of both sexes. 'A big plus for us,' Philip Hook said to me, 'was that the school was mixed. You don't get that slightly prissy all-girl thing.'

It helps that Lucie and Josie get on extremely well, share the same values, and have a great mutual respect for one another. 'Josie loves the school so much, she wants the staff to feel happy, and she's always happy to invest in beautiful new equipment. She makes it a very appealing place to work in.'

'I also feel it's vital,' Josie said to me, 'to send staff on day-long courses to refresh and extend their knowledge in their specialist areas. They love it and the children benefit hugely. Lucie is also a qualified school inspector – as I was once, too. Being a school inspector helps immeasurably in keeping you up to date with the latest rules and regulations; these change with monotonous regularity.'

What else are Lucie and Josie doing, I asked Lucie, to create even more opportunities for the children?

'We're doing lots,' she said. 'We now have themed subject days – a Maths Day, an Art Day, a Poetry Day, tomorrow we've got a Science Day, called "the Magic of Science". There'll be an egg race in the afternoon, when the children have to design a capsule for carrying an egg along, using their knowledge of pushes and pulls.' The children love these themed days and they raise the profile of that subject. 'On the Maths Day, they did problem-solving and maths investigations to find answers, and those answers gave them the number of grams they needed for the various ingredients in the cupcakes they made later in the day. A boy in Year 2 came up to me and said, "I never used to like maths but after that Maths Day, I love it."' On a day like this, the levels go up the school: the Reception class might be working with an

abacus while Year 6 will be putting algebraic problems into practice.

'If there isn't a club for a child's interest, I'll start one,' Josie declared many, many years ago; and this still stands. New after-school clubs come into being every year. 'We've got six or seven new ones,' Lucie told me: 'cricket club, pins and needles club, where the children sew beautiful items, touch-typing, maths investigation, Spanish, Mandarin – and we're hoping to start an Italian Club.' Also, hardly a day goes by without an educational trip, either in London or out of it. The coaches line up along The Vale, and the mass clunking of seatbelts is a sound you didn't hear in the 1980s.

Another thing Lucie is doing is trying to increase the school's links with the local community. 'Helping in the local council estate, working with the Royal Borough of Kensington and Chelsea in all sorts of ways. We're trying to tap into the borough. Because Cameron

House is an independent school, 'you have to reach out to them; they're not going to come and find you. But they've been really friendly and helpful. They've done scooter training with the children; we've now orchestrated school signage and zigzags on the street outside, good for safety. Yesterday Year 6 did a citizenship workshop with the Metropolitan Police.'

Our meeting ended; Lucie had a lot to do. 'The culture of kindness,' she told me, 'starts at the top and trickles down.' It's her job, she said, 'to breed kindness and energy in the team.'

Tuesday the 12th of July. End-of-year prize-giving at St Luke's Church in Sydney Street. Across the Royal Borough, mothers are deciding what to wear. Surely a day to get out of one's trousers into a skirt or dress. But which skirt or dress? Easier for the children who look effortlessly fetching in their school uniform: blue and white striped dresses with neatly tied bows at the back, and white Peter Pan collars piped in blue and white stripes, and white shirts and navy blue corduroy shorts for the boys. Fathers in their dark suits with bright ties make their way across London to St Luke's for the prompt 2pm start.

As Josie crosses the street towards the church's west front, I think of the Revd Niall Weir telling his first Walter Woodbine story in the rose garden to the side. Parents are arriving in droves. Josie's children, Lucy, Henry and Edward, are with us and I can see how proud they are of their mother for bringing this school into being.

We go into the church and are greeted by two children handing out programmes at the west door. A glimpse shows that this is going to be more than just a prize-giving. Someone is playing Beethoven's

Moonlight Sonata on the piano, but the sound is muffled by the chat of parents who all know each other and have lots to talk about. Conversations seem to be more vibrant than the usual suspicious 'So which senior schools are you considering?' kind.

Making my way towards the front pew I reach the realm of the children's pews and walk through a sea of pale blue and white, the sight of children of matching heights in matching uniforms. So many plaits...I think of the mothers who must plait their daughters' hair, day in, day out.

The person playing the *Moonlight* Sonata is Juliana Beekenkamp, the Head Girl, who, with the Head Boy James Pentland, showed me around the school a few weeks ago. Today is their last day at the school: Juliana is off to St Paul's, James to Latymer. Not an easy piece, that sonata, four sharps, a definite cut above *Für Elise*, and sensitively

For her encore, karate blackbelt Juliana Beekenkamp plays CHOPin!

played. This girl has also just achieved her karate black belt.

Before the programme begins I sit in a side chapel and have a chat with the author Kitty Aldridge, Mrs Mark Knopfler, mother of old girl Isabella and Katya (now in Class 2). 'The school offers a unique blend of friendliness, support, and opportunity for creativity,' she says. 'There's a complete absence of negative pressure. From the moment they arrive aged four, the children have the opportunity to try things out and try on personalities. They are vibrant and unafraid. I've been a parent here for eight years and I've never once seen a child afraid to express him- or herself or to be who they are. If a child is curious about something and there isn't a club for it, the school will create one. The children define the character of the school, not the other way round: that's unique.'

I slip back into my pew for the welcome from Lucie Moore, full of praise for the pupils' achievements over the year. Success, she says, is not about how far you've got but how far you've travelled since you began. She ends with a Dr Seuss quote: '*You have brains in your head. You have feet in your shoes. You can steer yourself any direction you choose.*'

We set off into a mini-concert. The first item is a Dutch tune played by the small orchestra of violins and flutes. The little violinist on the far left has his legs dangling off the chair. We in the front pew can't resist making 'Oh-how-sweet!' faces as we applaud. Then

the whole school stands up to sing the school song, composed by longtime friend of Cameron House, Sir David Willcocks CBE MC:

'Sing, sing, Cameronians, sing! Join in every girl and boy,
Sing for our future, sing for our school, Cameronians, sing
with joy.'

Behind me the plaited girls in Reception sing out lustily, knowing the words by heart. More pieces: songs conducted by the head of music Jonathan Bunney – an organist in his own right who plays all over the country in various cathedrals – who brings the best out of every voice. Then some readings, the microphone passed from child to child. Isabel Jackson plays charmingly on her recorder, James Pentland on his guitar.

On the white-clothed table behind, school cups are glinting, interspersed with pristine hardback books. Nearly time for the handing out of these prizes, in the centre of which stands the school mascot, a small squirrel called Bramble, wearing a Cameron House scarf with the school crest.

The guest of honour, Catriona Sutherland-Hawes, the registrar at Latymer School, stands up to speak. She's delighted to be welcoming three of the Cameron House leavers to Latymer in September. 'You're very lucky, being at Cameron House,' she tells the children. 'You probably know it, but just in case you don't…' Having the stability of this environment, she tells them, 'has allowed each of you to develop as a person.' She extols the virtues of co-education. 'Girls are good for boys, and boys for girls.'

try drawing it with your eyes closed or left handed, see what happens. Right, I'm off to make some waterbombs…

Sit down! Finish your book, then we can go & make waterbombs together.

Well done! Which one have you won?

It's the Alen-Buckley Spirit of Enquiry cup, I'm just seeing what's at the bottom, I heard a rattle.

Lucie announces the prizewinners. Every child in the school stands up as his or her name is announced: each one receives a certificate, so no one will go home with nothing.

To the right I see a familiar face: it's Sensei Lavender Ralston-Saul, the karate teacher who knocked on the door of the verger's cottage in 1983 and announced herself to Josie, in her pearls. She has driven from Somerset to be here and give the karate cup to its winner. She gives Josie a smile of deep affection. 'And the Arabella Ralston-Saul Karate Cup goes to...Juliana Beekenkamp.' Huge applause as a glowing Juliana and a delighted Lavender shake hands: the woman who helped the earliest Learning Tree children to grow in confidence through karate, and the high-achieving Juliana who has not allowed her part-deafness to mar her zest for life.

The form prizes are announced: three children in each class are awarded one. The children say 'thank you' and shake hands as they receive their prize from Catriona Sutherland-Hawes, and, if it's a book rather than a cup, they start reading it the moment they sit back down in their pew again. I can see Catriona, an avid reader herself obviously, having a quick look at each book before she parts with it.

Then come the cups: the Spirit of Enquiry Cup, donated by the Alen-Buckley family, the Lower School Art Prize donated by the Vaughan family, the Stanley Cup for Mathematics, donated by The Earl and Countess of Derby, so enormous that it brings forth a gasp from the whole school...these and many more are received by children, aware that the proud gaze (and perhaps also video camera) of their parents is upon them. Each of the leavers is given a fountain pen engraved with his or her name. As the chamber choir strikes up with Bob Chilcott's *Irish Blessing*:

> *'May the road rise up to meet you, may the wind be always at your back, may the sun shine warm upon your face, the rains fall soft upon your fields, and until we meet again may God hold you in the palm of your hand,'*

I rummage in my bag for a Kleenex – and I'm not even the mother of one of the leavers. Astonishing how quickly our children's childhoods pass.

189

Chapter 12

One Glorious Acacia Tree...

On a Tuesday afternoon in the spring term of 2012, Josie gave me a tour of Cameron House, from basement to top. I wanted her to show me exactly where those old food-lifts had been, which she had got rid of in the summer of 1986 in order to free up vital new square metres of space.

This tour took me – and I hope it now takes the reader – full circle, back to the beginning of the school's existence at 4 The Vale, which came directly out of The Learning Tree, which came directly out of the attic, which came directly out of the desk in the corridor, coming directly out of Josie's determination to bring her unique stamp to the world of education. Always, she has tried to banish the emotion of fear from the child's experience of school.

'In this corner,' she said, as we stood by the door to the garden, 'used to be the old school kitchens of The Vale school. There was a strong smell of fatty mince.' Josie did away with these kitchens straight away, preferring packed lunches, and shunning any possibility of a pervasive cabbagy smell wafting up through the house at 11am, which is such a vivid part of many of our memories of schooldays. (Why did they always start cooking the cabbage so early?)

Better get these cabbages on, Ethel. They need at least 3 hours of hard boiling

School dinners circa 1970

Where that old kitchen was, there is now a useful and recently installed downstairs loo in the corner. That, too, had a story to go with it – this time about the school inspectors and their box-ticking ways. 'The school inspector told me on Friday evening, in the Summary of Findings meeting, that we needed an additional loo down here,' Josie said, 'because the law had just changed. So, there and then, over that very weekend, I had this one put in. Our builders built it in 48 hours, over the weekend. But that wasn't quick enough for the inspectors. And because of that, they gave the school one black mark in an otherwise glowing report.' The injustice rankles.

Josie took me out into the padded garden playground and it was good to see, in her company, the balcony from which the snow had been generated by her on that December morning, the vertical magnetic chess set donated by the Stanley family, and the 'one glorious acacia

191

tree' behind which so many sticker books had been filled over the years, so many games played, so many swaps made. 'This garden was completely concrete when I arrived.' She showed me the music room in the school's converted garage. 'The outdoor music room means that children don't disturb the rest of the school while they make their first tentative noises on the violin or the flute – or noisier still, the trombone, chanter or bagpipes.'

As we went back into the building, we were greeted by numerous charming, polite children, who said to Josie, 'Thank you for the bookmark.' She had given every child a leather Cameron House bookmark to mark the Diamond Jubilee. The sense of a 'school family' was tangible.

In the little staff room there were signs of lunch brought in from the Bluebird: this is something Josie does for the staff every day – brings them a delicious lunch from a local delicatessen.

'Are you always having to get the builders in?' I asked.

'Always,' Josie said. 'Most summers, we have the scaffolding up.' She's undaunted by this fact, which would daunt many a householder. But she knows that the upkeep and continuous improvement of the building are of key importance.

'Are these Hunting McKinnon carpets?' I asked as we went upstairs. The carpets on the stairs had always interested me. They seemed to hark straight back to Josie's early childhood in a kilt at Columba Girls' College in Dunedin.

'No, they're Anderson carpets,' Josie said. 'They're unbelievably cosy and durable, and they absorb noise. And they make you feel as though you're in a house.' (The motto of Anderson Carpets is 'A reputation you can stand on since 1954.')

As we went upstairs we saw the head of music Jonathan Bunney

hearing a child read on a sofa on one of the landings in one of his spare moments. Jonathan is a fine organist, at St Giles-in-the-Fields, but he loves his four-day-a-week job here, he later told me as we had a chat by the piano in the room which triples up as music room, ballet room and dining-room. (The lunch ladies, also loyal and long-standing, were clearing away the spillage from the packed lunches.) 'Music complements so many different aspects of the children's education,' Jonathan said. 'It helps them with their listening skills, their creativity, their imagination, their confidence.' He is impressed by how quickly the children pick up songs, and by how good many of their voices are, and by how their confidence develops as they are encouraged to take part in choral and theatrical singing.

'That's Anna Monger,' Josie pointed out in one of the classrooms. 'She's the granddaughter of Rosemary Somers.' That was the woman I visited, whose son Mark had been rescued from paralysing dyslexia by

The Learning Tree over thirty years previously, and who herself now helps dyslexics, so inspired was she by what Josie did for Mark. 'And that's Dylan Pierce-Jones – his family has been connected to the school for sixteen years...there are four children.'

In every classroom there were two teachers – the teacher and the assistant. 'The ratio of children to teachers is about 7:1,' Josie said, 'which is pretty amazing, really.' We went up to the Year 1 classroom, and admired the view of the Chelsea roofscape out of the high windows. Here, the children had been creating watercolours of flowers which the specialist art teacher Nicki Whiteway had brought in from her garden. The paintings were impressive: Nicki is an inspirational art teacher, Josie said, who has been at the school for sixteen years. 'She really teaches the magical art of observation, the technique of painting and how to develop a child's unique style. The whole process of creating and developing art is terrific for self-esteem and confidence-building.'

Also in the Year 1 classroom was the teaching assistant Annie Honjo, who at the time of my visit was down to the last two in the shortlist for Teaching Assistant of the Year for the whole of London and the South East. As well as being a teaching assistant, she teaches Latin to Years 5 and 6. The parents at the school put her forward for this award.

In the corner was the food-lift's ghost: a separate area exactly the shape and size of a food-lift, which is now full from ceiling to floor, with pegs, coats, schoolbags, and books on shelves.

As we climbed to the top of the house, we passed a portable mural that Josie commissioned when she first moved into the verger's cottage. Trees, rabbits, bees, luscious flowers, the whole picture going down to ground level... 'You can pull something out to talk about at every level,' she told me. Always in her mind has been the shy, small, nervous child who might be walking up the stairs and might be put at ease by a passing wild animal to think about.

At the top of the house, with a bigger view of Chelsea chimneys, as well as the dome of the Oratory and the pinnacles of St Luke's, is the aforementioned ICT room, which was built in 1992. A technician was up there, tweaking laptops while the children were out.

'Do you like the colour of the walls?' Josie asked, as we went back downstairs, past a secluded desk where children who need learning support are given help with their reading and writing. The walls were pale yellow. 'I do like it,' I said, 'but I don't have a strong feeling about which colours are good to live and work with.'

'Don't you?' she asked. 'I do – a very strong feeling. I always have had. Pale yellow is a "think" colour. It opens up the mind.'

Thinking about children and how to help them reach their potential has been a constant in Josie's life. Her old friend Jane Emerson, the Headmistress of Emerson House, talked to me about this instinct to help children. She – Jane – has it too. 'There's a personality type called "the helper". It's a natural instinct and inclination.' Jane added quickly and laughingly, 'It doesn't mean you're particularly good or anything! We just seem to have the same values, the same moral belief, and the same mission that we can't stop.'

If Josie so much as hears of any child who has lost his or her way, Jane said, she will not rest until she has done all she can to help. She'll make telephone calls, she'll think of everyone she knows who might be able to help.

Bearing this in mind it seems natural that Josie should have been for many years associated with two charities that help disadvantaged children. One of them is First Story, which raises funds to employ authors to go into schools and encourage children to write stories and poems. At the end of each term an anthology of the children's work is published. Some of it is extremely good – as I can say from first-hand, having been to three First Story events and heard William Fiennes and Katie Waldegrave, the founders, reading aloud to the audience some of the children's stories.

The other charity is The Art Room, similar to First Story except that it's an art-based rather than word-based charity. It was founded in Oxford by Juli Beattie. As Josie explained, 'Juli takes in children in danger of being excluded. They have tea and toast and chats and they do artwork together. It's a moment of peace in the children's lives. There's now an Art Room in London too, and there are more on the horizon, including one in Edinburgh.'

Josie gives to these charities, and she's forging links to the Art Room from Cameron House, with fund-raising initiatives such as the 'coffee-cup fund' (dreamed up by a girl in Year 6 at the school, Luna Middleton-Roy) whereby the money that might have been spent on the after-drop-off cup of coffee is donated. 'Our children realise that other children aren't as fortunate. We want to reach out and help, but the whole thing has to be about forging links, opening eyes.'

Chapter 13
Mothers, Sea Creatures and Confidence

The overall winner of the adjective-most-used-by-parents-to-describe-Cameron-House is 'nurturing'. 'Caring for and encouraging the growth or development of' is the dictionary definition of the word. It's clear that the school does nurture whatever talent the children show, be it in sport or art or karate or drama – or be it a low-key talent that other schools, perhaps, would not bother to celebrate. 'There was a certificate for colouring-in, in the reception class,' Cosi Middleton-Roy (mother of Luna and India) told me.

Of the school staff, Cosi said, 'They go the extra mile every time.' She singled out the head of music, Jonathan Bunney – 'such a kind man, utterly passionate, finds music that really suits the children' – and Hugh the sports teacher – 'who gives up every weekend for sports clubs' and is revered by children and parents alike.

And Lucie? 'She loves to see the children becoming more confident,' Cosi said. 'My eldest daughter was very shy when she arrived at the school, almost introverted, but Lucie has helped her to blossom. The whole school has.' Cosi also spoke highly of the

learning support that the school offers. What's especially good about it, she said, is that the children are hardly aware that they're having 'learning support' help at all. 'There's absolutely no stigma attached. You might be getting extra help if you're especially gifted, or if you're dyslexic or have other learning difficulties. You might dip in and out of it. The children often don't even know it's happening – they just think, "Another nice tutor is teaching me."'

'One thing you notice about having four children,' said Yvette Pierce-Jones, whose children Barney, Agnes, Rufus and Dylan have all been at Cameron House, 'is that they're all very different: but although one is good at one thing and another is good at another, all mine have come away thinking they're good at something. I've

noticed this in other children at the school, not just my own.'

Simone Lehndorff, the mother of Philip, Valeska, Cosima and Victoria, who have all been at or are still at the school, said, 'I like the fact that you can drop your children into the classroom – you don't have to leave them at the school gate. I'm forever bringing a violin or something in, that someone has forgotten, and the school always welcomes the parents, any time.'

I asked her about the international feel of the school. At Wendy Miller's lunch party, I noticed that a number of the parents present spoke with American or Canadian accents. 'That's the nature of Chelsea,' Simone Lehndorff said. Simone (herself German) celebrates the multi-national aspect of the school – 'but it's sad when families relocate back to their native country. Your child might find his or her best friend is suddenly gone. That's the downside. But that's the nature of London life today.' However, the upside is they can visit friends abroad in the holidays. A group of thirtysomethings is holding a Cameron House reunion in New York and one in Chicago. All keep in touch via social media such as Facebook.

The mothers I spoke to said they thought it was good for children to get to know people from different countries. Mary-Margaret Lhuilier, mother of Isabella (Head Girl 2012), said wistfully, 'I'm looking at secondary schools and I don't see such a big mix of nationalities.' Tracey Good and Brittan Chepak told me about the previous year's Spring Fair with its 'Around the World in Eighty Days' theme, in which different objects and costumes from all over the world were shown.

It's part of the culture, these mothers said, for parents to be deeply involved in school life. The school's bake-sale tradition has been further bolstered by American parents, renowned for their muffin- and brownie-making. But it's not just the baking, it's the general expectation of being there, being involved, enhancing the school lives of the children by raising money to help extra things to happen – such as for there to be an ice-cream van at Sports Day giving out free ice-creams to the children – as well as keeping parents' morale and blood sugar up with Pimm's, strawberries and shortbread. All over the Millennium Arena on Sports Day, you can see pinstriped suited fathers sipping Pimm's with strawberries and mint leaves – one of Josie's favourite sights of the school year.

I detected a slight air of sea-creature-costume angst at the FoCH lunch party. It was Monday, and the mothers were aware that by Friday their children would need to go to school dressed up. Alliteratively, Mulberry House had a medieval theme, Carlyle House had a countries

In my day
I could run 100
metres in around
10 seconds and do a
sub 4 minute mile...

theme, and Sydney had a sea creatures theme. No doubt which of those was the most challenging. The mothers of children in Sydney were fretting about scales and tentacles.

On Friday I turned up at the school door at 8.30am, curious to see the results. Lucie was in the entrance hall, wearing a hat which managed to combine on its brim the three themes of medieval, countries and sea creatures. On the doorstep, families were arriving, children excited, parents putting last-minute touches to hat-angles. The pouring rain was failing to dampen spirits and actually seemed to suit the sea creatures. As the children came in, each one shook hands with Lucie (as happens every day) and she greeted each one by name and commented enthusiastically on their costumes. They all smiled and the smallest ones beamed with pride. I saw what the parents meant about being welcomed into the building. Unlike other schools, where parents are not invited to step over the threshold except at parents' evenings, here they uninhibitedly step inside. Mothers (not all, but some) accompanied their children up the stairs, chatting as they went.

I noted that the best way to do a sea creature costume is to use a shallow upturned plastic bowl to go on the head, and have long dangly silver ribbons or strips of paper hanging from it. An instant octopus or jellyfish. Others had made a two-sided shark out of rubbery paper and were wearing it as a headdress. As for the countries, we had fine examples, including a Statue of Liberty and a Scotsman in a kilt. And there were a great many knights. It was going to be a good day. Lucie's energy fizzed. I wished I could stay for the day rather than having to go out, like all the parents, into the damp morning.

Vicarious pleasure: that's what parents become good at taking. You learn when to back off. It's the children's turn to be at school and

you must leave them there, glimpsing the atmosphere for ten seconds as you say goodbye but knowing that they are in good hands, in a place that will help to form them and instil in them the values you treasure.

Sometimes, as on that morning, you have a strong desire to bottle the atmosphere and bring it home with you to take out and sniff in dark or lonely times to come. Do the children have any idea how lucky they are? Some have a sense of it. But you wouldn't want them to brood on abstracts like that. They're too busy living their childhoods, day by day, term by term, time flying past, all turning into a blur.

What will they remember? If you read the 'Some Old Cameronians' chapter after this one, you'll see the varied memories that pupils carry with them in adult life. Beneath all their pinpointed specific memories there's a rich seam of general happiness – an overriding memory of having been nurtured and fulfilled in a school which looked for the best in them and brought it out.

At the Cameron House prize-giving and concert in July 2013, Michael Morpurgo OBE, FRSL, FKC (the third British Children's Laureate) was the guest of honour. First there was a short concert, which included Old Cameronian Lachlan Grassie (dazzling on the bagpipes) piping the children and staff into church, and then splendid musical items by the pupils. To a packed St Luke's Church, Michael read one of his stories aloud: *The Rainbow Bear*. Parents, staff and children listened in rapt silence – not only because the story was riveting, but also because Morpurgo had warned us that when he finished he was going to pick a random person from the audience and ask him or her to state the story's moral. 'I was a teacher once,' he said, with some sternness.

The story was of a polar bear who sees a rainbow and suddenly wishes he could be not white any more, but rainbow-coloured instead. His wish is granted but this does not bring him the happiness he longs for. He becomes much too visible and is captured by men and taken to a zoo, where he longs for his wild white home.

Morpurgo read the story with vigorous crescendos and decrescendos. This was not your usual prize-giving speech. There we all were, completely caught up in Rainbow Bear's plight. When at last

Be yourself, children,
and don't let anyone
tell you otherwise

Rainbow Bear sees sense and goes back to being a contented white polar bear in a white wilderness, there was a collective sigh of relief.

Who was going to be plucked out of the audience to tell the moral of this tale? Some of us hid behind pillars, but there was an enthusiastic show of hands among the children.

'You,' said Michael Morpurgo, choosing Imogen White, who had just performed a stunning solo rendition of *You Raise Me Up*, the song by the Secret Garden duo. 'Are you the one who sang to us so beautifully?'

Imogen hit the nail on the head, moral-of-story-wise. 'I think it's really that you should be yourself,' she said.

'Quite right,' said Michael Morpurgo. 'Be yourself. Out in the world there are lots of things encouraging you to be not-yourself. Don't be taken in by them.'

Being yourself – being your best self – is a moral totally in tune with the Cameron House philosophy of education and of life.

Chapter 14

Some Old Cameronians... and what they did next

All the following entries were accurate at the time of writing, but life moves on and some may well have changed.

LUKE ALEN-BUCKLEY

After Cameron House Luke went on to Trevor Roberts, then to Ampleforth, and then to the Edinburgh College of Art. 'I did a year there before going to study Physics at Heriot-Watt University in Edinburgh.' Quite a change. 'I did well in the end, but I did prefer the concepts to the nitty-gritty.' After university he moved to the USA to set up a sun-cream company, which didn't work but was 'a lot of fun'. He came back to London and worked in the financial world, for Musst Investments. When we spoke, he was planning to move to Milan to work for another company.

Most vivid CH memories: 'I was very dyslexic. I used to have remedial lessons before school. Cameron House gave me lots of help all the way through. Parents would come in and do reading sessions with us. It was a very friendly and homely school and I had a lot of fun there.'

VERITY BARD

Verity works for the company Abbott Mead Vickers BBDO as a television producer, making commercials. After leaving Cameron House she went to Queensgate, then to Mander Portman Woodward. In her gap year she taught English in Vietnam, then she went to Nottingham University to read English and American Studies.

Most vivid CH memories: 'Of all my years at school, the fondest memories are of Cameron House. I loved Jane Emmett: she had the lovely combination of being severe at times but also incredibly warm and nurturing and fun. The school had a real warmth and energy and that came from Josie and Jane. I remember we did tie-dyeing in Art, and we all put on our tie-dyed T-shirts and went to the park across the road to have our photos taken.'

LUKE BATT

Luke is a professional musician: a singer-songwriter and performer in his own right as well as a published songwriter for Sony Music. 'I have an album I'm just about to start promoting,' he told me. 'Self-written, words and music. It's called *Outside In*.' Luke enjoys focusing on writing, production and performing. He toured for a year and a half, doing support tours for other artists, but decided he needed to take a break and concentrate on his new album.

Most vivid CH memory: The monkey with lollipop paws, in *The Dong with the Luminous Nose*, written especially for the school by his father Mike Batt LVO.

AMADEA BENTHEIM

After leaving Cameron House, Amadea went on to St Paul's Girls' School and then to read History of Art at Emmanuel College, Cambridge. She is working for a hedge fund as an analyst – 'It's my first job, and it's been great so far. I never wanted to work in the art world. I always said I wanted to be a barrister. I remember saying it to my friend Hayley Batt when we were in the playground at Cameron House, aged about seven, and it was the first time she'd come across the word "barrister". Maybe that's something I'll approach later in life. I did some internships and then was offered this lovely job.'

Most vivid CH memories: 'It was a really magical place to go to school. I loved the fact that it was mixed-ability but everyone was taught to do the very best they possibly could. I wanted to work hard and to push myself: it was cool to do that.

'I loved the school trips: to France, to Cornwall. There used to be a yearly trip across to France for the day on a ferry, and we used to buy trinkets and practise our rudimentary French. I remember the end-of-year discos. There was a dance competition in the playground. As a class we'd choose a song to dance to. Embarrassing to recollect, but I don't think we were at all embarrassed at the time. Britney Spears was a popular choice.

'There were some real characters in our year. There was one boy in our class who strapped stink bombs onto the bottom of his shoes and said he'd stamp his feet if we didn't have Art before Science.'

JESS BONHAM

Now in her early thirties, Jess is working as a freelance still-life photographer, taking photographs for the advertising and editorial sides of magazines such as *Vogue* and *The Gourmand*.

Jess went on to More House, then to Sherborne, then to MPW for A-Levels. She did a foundation course at Camberwell College of Arts before studying illustration at the University of Brighton. Working as first assistant to the photographer Julian Broad, she learned the fundamentals of photography.

Most vivid CH memories: 'Dissecting a bull's eye: we had an exotic science teacher, Carina [Greenwood], with tumbling corkscrew hair. I remember some children having to go out of the classroom to take a breather during the dissection, but I loved it.' Another teacher, Emma, gave Jess's mother her goldfish – and astonishingly, one of those goldfish is still alive. 'It must be 13 years old now. It's completely blind and white. It must have nine lives: it's jumped out of its bowl on a number of occasions but has always survived. The fish that will never die.'

Karate with Lavender was a major part of Jess's CH life; she carried on training with Lavender till the age of 20, and became a black belt.

KATIE BONHAM

As well as being trained up by her father Nick Bonham to be an auctioneer (Bonham's is no longer a family business, though it retains the name, but Nick Bonham still works in the charity auction sector), Katie is setting up her own business. 'It's a singles venture: I'm building an online dating website, called Montyslondon.com, and we organise singles parties too. We're trying to change the face of online dating. The idea is to attract fun, colourful, young, interesting people. The profiles, instead of being purely written ones, will be built out of photographs of you and of things you like, places you like, YouTube videos of music you like, and so on: more like a visual sketchbook of you.'

Most vivid CH memories: 'I remember my desk, with the little lid you used to lift up, and all the books inside. I remember the little cloakroom where we used to keep our lunchboxes. Lunchtimes were great: I loved my lunchbox. The teachers were lovely, young, fun, good, happy people. I particularly remember one called Georgina [Stokely]. Jane Emmett was amazing: smiley, happy, cuddly, awesome.'

I have literally NO idea where she gets it from

MILO BROCKWAY

Milo is now a helicopter pilot. For a while he worked in Aberdeen, flying people to oil rigs, and then he worked for the Coastguard in the Shetland Islands, but now he's working in Norfolk, flying people out to gas rigs – only 40 or 50 miles offshore, unlike the oil rigs which are 200 miles away. 'A one-hour return trip, quite an easy job,' Milo says. 'Since I was six I've always wanted to be a pilot. I just followed my dream.' After Cameron House he went to Ibstock Place, and then on to Hurtwood, and then straight to flight training at the British training school in Florida.

Most vivid CH memories: 'We had a den behind that big tree in the playground. Not much space to make a den there, but we did. Getting the coach to Battersea Park for games. Going to the Chelsea Library and sitting on beanbag cushions reading cartoons. I really loved that. Instead of reading at our desks in the classroom, there we were at a library, on beanbags.'

VICTORIA BRUDENELL

Victoria is working for a business investigations firm, investigating business frauds. After Cameron House she went on to Heathfield and then read Russian at Jesus College, Cambridge. I'm using my Russian in this job. Most of the companies we investigate are Russian ones.'

Most vivid CH memories: 'Life behind the tree in the playground. A lot of pog-swapping: those were little plastic discs that we swapped around. Also I remember being the lion in *The Wizard of Oz*. That was the peak of my dramatic career. I also remember being in *The BFG* and being taller than the boy who was playing the part of *The BFG*.'

ALEXANDRA COOPER

Alexandra went on to Wycombe Abbey, then read History at Edinburgh, and then did a Masters in History of Art, specialising in Indian and Persian painting, at the School of Oriental and African Studies in London. Now she is working for a leading dealer of Islamic and Indian art as a specialist and researcher.

Most vivid CH memories: 'I remember the playground with the tree that we used to play and gossip behind, walking to games lessons along the Kings Road, and trying to whisper on the "Quiet Street".'

EDWARD COOPER

After graduating from the University of St Andrews in 2005 with a degree in Ancient History, Edward trained as a lawyer. He is now working for the law firm Taylor Wessing as a real-estate litigator. Married and living in London, he is 'trying to scale back the dangerous sports': while at St Andrews he was president of the Mountaineering Club, and his most notable mountaineering achievement was to make the first-ever ascent of a 6,000-metre peak in the Himalayas – 'not super-technical, but very remote, in Kashmir.'

Most vivid CH memories: 'I remember the school plays. I was never very gifted in drama, but I did have a semi-main part in one of the plays. I was a character called Gluck the Wise. I remember during the dress rehearsal the whole cast was sitting backstage and the teacher said to us all, "Now, you've really got to pull your socks up. This has got to get better." All of us – every single one – actually pulled our socks up. We thought that was what she meant.'

SAM CROSFIELD

Sam is now a professional gardener with a prized Kew Diploma. Five hundred applicants applied for fourteen places to be accepted onto the coveted three-year Kew Diploma course, and Sam won a place. His experience of going from the Lycée to The Learning Tree taught him to be appreciative of the good fortune which life can bring. When I spoke to him he was working for a garden company but hoping to set up his own business.

Sam also takes evening French lessons once a week for two

oui, heureusement j'ai les doigts verts

hours – and his stamina for this shows how far he has come since the blocked days of language-learning (even his own language) of his early childhood. He now enjoys reading 'but I need to be in total silence in order to read and fully comprehend what I'm reading.'

Most vivid CH memory: 'The padded playground when the school moved to The Vale. Hours of fun, and a break from looking at a book.'

ALEXANDRA FINLAY

Alexandra runs her own footwear and accessory business for men, called Fin's For Him. Having begun her career working for another company, Alexandra longed to have her own business – 'I wanted to put my own name above the door of something,' as she put it – 'and men's shoes seemed as good an idea as any. It's been super-fun and amazing and I've enjoyed every minute of it.' She went on from Cameron House to St Paul's.

One of many things she loves about her work is that the headquarters of Fin's For Him is on King's Road, round the corner from Cameron House. She walks past her old school every morning and notices the scooters. 'This is my stomping ground,' she says.

Most vivid CH memory: 'Playing the part of Little Orphan Annie in the school play in my last year. My acting was questionable but I certainly had the voice of an angel: that I can confirm. My rendition of the song *Maybe* had a large portion of the audience in tears.'

TiFFANY GooDALL

Tiffany now works at the Bluebird, heading its events management team, and she is the author of two cookbooks, *From Pasta to Pancakes: The Ultimate Student Cookbook* (a bestseller, published in seven languages) and *The First Flat Cookbook*. 'I'm still living in my first flat,' she told me, 'with my first cat and my boyfriend.'

Most vivid CH memories: 'I remember Jane Emmett being brilliant: firm but kind. We really respected her, we really wanted to please her.' Packed lunches: 'A sandwich, some carrot sticks, a bit of chocolate. If Dad was making the sandwiches, it was white bread; if Mum was making them, it was brown bread.'

ATTY GORDON-LENNOX

Atty is training to be a psychotherapist at the University of San Francisco – her second master's degree. Her first degree was in Russian and History at UCL. She worked in Moscow, in advertising, for a while, then came back to London, where she worked for the magazine *Intelligent Life* and had a column in the motor sport section of the *Daily Telegraph*. A bout of itchy feet took her to Argentina on a whim. There she did Thai massage. Then she did a master's degree in Women's Spirituality at the Institute of Transpersonal Psychology in California. 'My thesis was on the concept of female authority, and, writing that, I realised I wanted to be a psychotherapist working with women. I'm interested in the different ways women can come into a more powerful place within themselves.'

Most vivid CH memories: 'I remember Cameron House being this amazing place where children could express who they really were. Studying psychology now, I think, "Wow, that was an amazingly progressive institution." If you wanted to wear the boys' uniform, that was fine. There was none of that "girls at one end of the room, boys at the other" thing. We were all good friends. I got the biggest shock going on to an all-girls boarding school afterwards. That was much more precious, much more "girly". At Cameron House you could show up as who you were. For a child I think that's a wonderful thing to be able to do.'

CLEMMIE HAMBRO

After Cameron House, Clemmie went on to Cobham Hall, and then read English at the University of West England. After a 'short and unfruitful stint as an actress' she became a writer, writing lifestyle and travel pieces for magazines.

After getting married and having her first baby, she says, 'I went to the English Gardening School as I found myself in possession of an unruly garden on Exmoor, which I had no idea what to do with except pull out nettles. I studied there for two years, during which I had another baby and miraculously became the garden columnist for *The Lady* magazine, which I did blissfully for the next three years.'

Clemmie now writes for the American gardening website Gardenista – but 'recently not so much as we've been on a sabbatical (or a sort of mad gap year) in the Bahamas for the last seven months, basically living on the beach.'

She is married to Orlando Fraser and they have three daughters, and live in London and Exmoor.

CHARLIE HAMILTON

Charlie spent three years at Cameron House before going on to Ludgrove, and then to Radley, and then to Exeter University where he read Classics and Ancient History. 'Not the most vocational of subjects,' he says. 'After Exeter I went to the Cass Business School in London and did a master's degree in Real Estate.'

Most vivid CH memories: 'I remember a rather bizarre playground lined with green padded plastic, a kind of lunatic asylum for children. I remember us all rushing out and screaming at the top of our lungs for fifteen minutes before going back in for lessons. I remember a street called "Quiet Street" which we weren't allowed to talk in as we walked to the Chelsea Baths for swimming. Apparently the residents had got annoyed at our noise. And I seem to remember building a volcano out of bicarbonate of soda.'

MALCOLM HAMILTON

After Cameron House, Malcolm went on to Ludgrove and then to Eton. Now he's at Trinity College Dublin, studying Economics and Politics, and at the time of talking to me he was in his year out, studying at the prestigious Sciences Po in Paris and loving living in that city, near the Boulevard St Germain. 'I had the choice between the university of Barbados or Paris and I chose Paris. The right choice, I think. I'm brushing up on my French, too.' He hopes to work for Jardines in Hong Kong after university.

Most vivid CH memories: 'I remember once a year we had to dress up as a character from a book. My mother and I would take it incredibly seriously and make fabulous costumes. One year we made a car called "Elf 64" out of cardboard, which I sat inside and went all the way to school in.' The family lived in Carlyle Square, so not too far away for that journey in cardboard, but quite far for the family pet. 'I used to walk our hamster to school. He had a little ball which he kicked along the pavement. I don't think he could manage the whole journey. We had to pick him up halfway and carry him.'

KIRSTEN HAMILTON-SMITH

After leaving Cameron House, Kirsty went to More House, then to Bradfield, and then to Newcastle University where she read Economics and Sociology. 'I landed in Singapore where I've been for four years, working for Rothschild's Bank. I left in March and am now spending as much time as I can travelling until my next job starts.' When in London, Kirsty still lives near Cameron House and 'I love walking past, seeing what pictures they've got on the walls.'

Most vivid CH memories: 'Karate was a major part of my life. Sensei Lavender was a fantastic karate teacher, amazing, inspiring. I remember learning loads and loads of poems which we had to recite. And I remember the school plays.'

MIRANDA HILLS

After leaving Francis Holland, Miranda read Archaeology at Durham University and now works in the Alps as a manager for VIP Ski. She is in Val d'Isère for six months of the year overseeing three groups of chalets. 'I'm in charge of staff well-being.'

Most vivid CH memories: 'Being in Year 2 with the wonderful Becky [Briscoe] as our teacher, in the top classroom in the eaves. I loved Becky: I really cared what she felt and had a real eagerness to please her. Rachel [Shaw] was another lovely teacher. The staff at that school didn't just "clock" a problem, they really acted on it and supported you. Also being Fat Sam in *Bugsy*: though I was slightly offended at being cast as a boy. I remember my brother being a monk and a rat. Clearly the Hillses aren't given to dramatics.'

SABINE HOOK

Sabine has been teaching in a primary school in Ealing, heading the Foundation Stage. She got an English degree at Durham University, and then went on to do teacher training at the Institute of Education in London. She taught at the International School in Cairo and also at a Church of England primary school near Holland Park.

When I spoke to her she was getting ready for her wedding in Kent in July 2012: and the priest taking the wedding was to be the Very Revd Derek Watson, who had been the Rector of St Luke's Church in Chelsea during Sabine's time at Cameron House, and with whom she and her family had kept closely in touch ever since.

Most vivid CH memories: 'A fantastic American teacher called Douglas [Tate], with Beach Boy blond hair. He taught sport and Latin. He had an amazing way of teaching us the conjugations. He marched round the classroom carrying a metre stick, and we all followed him as if he was the Pied Piper – all chanting, "I am! You are! He, She, It is! We are! You are! They are!" and then in Latin, "*Sum! Es! Est! Summus! Estis! Sunt!*" I've never forgotten those verbs, thanks to Douglas.'

Second most vivid memory: Being taken on a class walk round Chelsea by 'lovely teacher Emily [Cotterell]', and being shown all kinds of hidden corners which the children didn't know about, such as the Moravian cemetery. 'She pointed out what some of the buildings in Chelsea used to be – and when I go past now I still remember, "That's the building which used to be a dairy."'

EDMUND HOWARD

Edmund now works for Asylum Records in Kensington, which is part of Atlantic Records. He finds artists and helps them make their recordings, advising them on which songs to include, track-listing etc. 'Ed Sheeran is one of my biggest artists,' he said. 'I found him and brought him into the company. We made an album together and now he's doing pretty well both at home and abroad.'

After CH, Edmund went on to Worth, and then to New College, Oxford, where he read French and Italian.

Most vivid CH memories: 'The padded playground, everything being quite small, the packed lunches, football in the park, the services at St Luke's – and making good friends.'

OLIVER MOSLEY

When I spoke to him, Oliver was in his gap year after Eton before going to St John's College, Cambridge to read Politics. He was working as a researcher at the House of Commons, in the office of Crispin Blunt, MP for Reigate. 'I'm his second Westminster secretary. I have to answer emails and research policies, and I'm also the admin person for the Kaleidoscope Trust, of which he's the Chair.'

Most vivid CH memories: 'My Reception teacher, Ali Brumby, was fantastic. I remember I went through a few days of bad behaviour, and she picked up on it quickly. She took me out one playtime and asked what was wrong, and she helped me out of trouble. That kind of thing might not have been picked up on by some teachers. She's still friends with my parents, many years later.'

SARAH NALLE

Sarah is working for the publishers Simon & Schuster in New York City. She is still great friends with Hayley Batt, who is also living in New York, and whom she remembers on her (Sarah's) first day at Cameron House asking her to play Izzy-Wizzy – 'and having just arrived from the US I had no idea what that was.' (Basically it involves spinning round and round and round until you're so dizzy that you fall over.) After Cameron House Sarah went to Godolphin and Latymer, and then the family moved back to the United States. She went to the University of Pennsylvania.

Most vivid CH memories: Discovering Harry Potter before the book was famous. Going on a Form 6 trip to Cornwall and surfing in the freezing waves. Doing the mother-and-daughter's race on Sports Day, mother's and daughter's ankles roped together.

SAM REID

After leaving Cameron House Sam went on to Ludgrove and then to Eton. In his gap year he came back to Cameron House to be a Class 3 assistant and to help with the sports. 'That was a huge part of my growing up,' he said. 'Being given the responsibility for looking after children made me a more mature person.' He then did a history degree at Oxford Brookes. Now he is enjoying working for a London company called Mindshare, doing sponsorship consultancy, helping brands to decide on their sponsorship strategy.

Most vivid CH memory: 'Playing a lot of football in Battersea Park. My family started the Reid Cup for football – and I won it in its first year. That wasn't supposed to be the aim of the game.' Sam played football for Oxford Brookes when he was at university, and said, 'I wouldn't have played as much sport if it hadn't been for Cameron House. Sport is the thing I'll take away with me.'

FREDERICK VAN DE WYCK

Frederick works for Goldman Sachs, as a strategist, or 'number cruncher'. After Cameron House he went on to Westminster Under School, then to Westminster, then to Oxford where he read Mathematics, and then to Harvard where he did a PhD in Mathematics.

Josie picked up on this natural propensity for maths when Frederick came to the school for his assessment aged five and walked straight across the room to inspect the abacus.

Most vivid CH memory: Frederick remembers that everyone had a drawing of a rocket to colour in, in stages. 'When you'd learned the next times-table you were allowed to colour in the next bit of the rocket.' The children found this motivating: 'We all wanted to be the first to finish our rocket.'

HENRY VAUGHAN

'I started as a very unintellectual and incompetent individual at Cameron House (I was much the better when I left); then I went to Ludgrove School for five years, then to Radley for the next five years, and from there to Bristol University where I read Sociology and came out with a 2:1 (just!). Now I am working in finance, specifically in foreign exchange broking at a company called Ebury Partners where I am hoping to build a long and successful career!'

ALEXIS WATKINS

Alexis is a qualified accountant, but at the time of speaking he had just left an accountancy job and was hoping to do 'something more creative', such as voice-overs for animation. He is also an artist, working in coloured pencils. His drawings are in vibrant colours and he particularly enjoys painting wildlife. A recent commission was to create a picture to hang on the bedroom wall of a child whom some friends had adopted from Guatemala. 'I made a picture of the birds, flowers and wildlife of Guatemala to remind her of the country where she was born.'

Most vivid CH memory: 'The green padded playground, and the massive acacia tree growing out of it which we used to climb.'

JASPER WHITFIELD

Jasper is now an art dealer working for his family's company, Whitfield Fine Art in Mayfair, one of the world's leading Old Masters galleries, specialising in 17th- and 18th-century Italian and Northern European painting. He has been there since graduating from university, where he read Politics.

Most vivid CH memories: 'Our fencing classes in the lunch room. I remember standing in lines, lunging at each other with our foils. That was fun. I still like walking past Cameron House. I always look through the windows to see if I can still see my coat peg.'

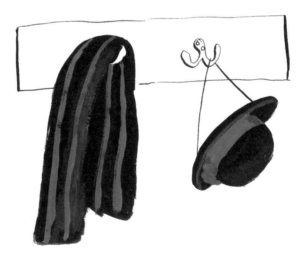

Acknowledgements

We would like to express our deep gratitude to all those who have given generously of their time to be interviewed for this book. Every reminiscence, from those of the earliest pupils and their teachers and parents to those of current ones, has added to the story of Cameron House. Special thanks to: Gilly and Chris Ashcroft, Katrina ffiske, Malcolm Garner, Shelley Griffiths-Shiels, Zebedee Helm, Clare Hill, Wendy Hutchinson, Ben Johnston, Brian Leathard, Brian MacReamoinn, Robert and Claudia Maxtone Graham, Lucie Moore, Philippa Perry, Katie Rockley, Malcolm Sadler, Amanda Smith, Dave Walker, Derek Watson, Sheila Watson, Niall Weir and all at Daunt Books.

Josie Cameron Ashcroft would like to thank: all the pupils, staff and parents of Cameron House School, past and present; The Friends of Cameron House Association; The Cameron House Charitable Foundation Trustees; and those who have taught and worked at the school during this academic year (2013–2014): Madeleine Balcar, Marc Bengry, Oribell Botero, Kimberley Boyle, Jonathan Bunney, Julie Chubb, Alisa Driscoll-Dutch, Tracey Ellerby, Hania Felt, Hugh Freeland, Suzanne Haigh, Amy Hayes, Melissa Healy, Imogen Hill, Dorothy Ind, Nariman Jeddi, Ann Jordan, Nils Klofver, Edward Lewis, Garth Lombard, Mary-Anne Malloy, Clare Moujaes, Yolanda Petronelli, Mary Pimlott, Sian Rhiannon Prosser, Dianne Redbond, Tim Short, Olivia Smithies, Vania Stankov, Jennifer Trott, Nicki Whiteway and Annie Worlledge.

Index

DA MIHI SAPIENTIAM: GIVE ME WISDOM